TYPE A Christian

TRANSFORMING PERSONALITY TRAITS
INTO FRUITFUL GROWTH

AUTUMN HOOVER

Type A Christian: Transforming Personality Traits into Fruitful Growth.

Book design: Matías Baldanza, for Chasing Kites Publishing.
Cover design: Christina Thomas

ISBN (paperback): 978-0-9997356-4-0

Type A Christian

TRANSFORMING PERSONALITY TRAITS INTO FRUITFUL GROWTH

AUTUMN HOOVER

CONTENTS

Dedication 1

Preface & Testimony 3

Introduction 13

CHAPTER ONE
Personality Types 19

CHAPTER TWO
Personality Quiz 37

CHAPTER THREE
Type A Personality Benefits 79

CHAPTER FOUR
Type A Personality Health
Risks & Coping Strategies 109

CHAPTER FIVE
Type A Traits vs. Fruit of the Spirit 165

Notes 195

Acknowledgments 203

About the Author 207

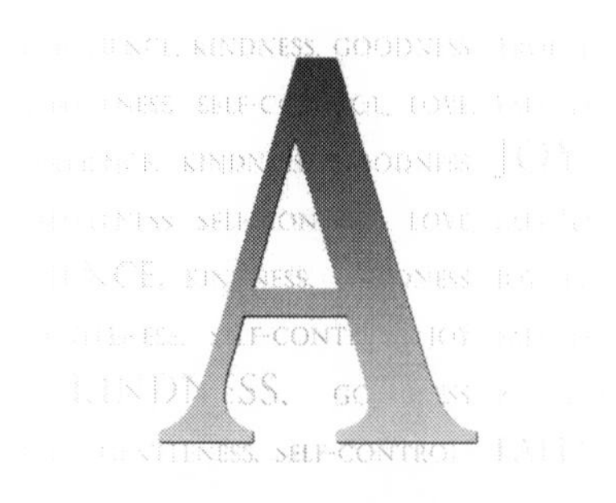

DEDICATION

First and foremost, I give praise to my Heavenly Father who provided the idea for this book and encouraged me throughout this entire process. I could never have written this book without the guidance of the Holy Spirit who lives inside of me. I am thankful for God's grace and the gift of eternal salvation through the death and resurrection of His Son, Jesus Christ.

To my parents—Bill and Sandy Johnson—you both ensured church was a priority as well as maintaining an active prayer life. George and I knew the importance of working hard first and then relaxing on the beach while eating endless crab legs! Thank you both for modeling a servant's heart and for all of the love and support you continue to provide.

To my husband of fifteen years—Rob—I am extremely proud of you for answering your call into the ministry. I know our family will be blessed solely by your leadership and commitment in serving the Lord. You have exceeded my expectations by being a wonderful husband and father. You have left such a legacy to your students and players in serving as a mentor and coach. And now you get to inspire others by using your spiritual gifts to tell others of Jesus.

To the little girl who calls me *"Momma"*—Reese—you are the answer to my prayers and proof of my faithfulness. I love your overwhelming commitment to the Lord. I am also proud of your confession of faith at such a young age, and I am truly inspired by your spiritual maturity—and you're not even ten years old! I continue to pray for your hearing, your health, and your safety as well as a God-fearing husband who will care for you in the future, just like your daddy takes care of me, but I must apologize now for your many inherited Type A traits that you already exhibit!

To my family—I am blessed to have many relatives who have put God first, which is something I know is not the norm. To my Mamaw Patsy who is in her eighties and still makes the best chicken 'n dumplings—you are the best example I have in being a selfless servant of Christ. Many thanks to my in-laws—David and Andi Hoover—who have encouraged me along the way and who also serve as Reese's private taxi service! To my brother and in-laws who blessed me with four other children to love as my own—I have enjoyed being 'Aunt Autie' to your kiddos. Drew, Abbey, Riley, and Logan—I am so proud of each of you, as well as the differences that make you unique. To all my relatives living in various states—no one knows the bond we have with one another. I love you all.

Autumn

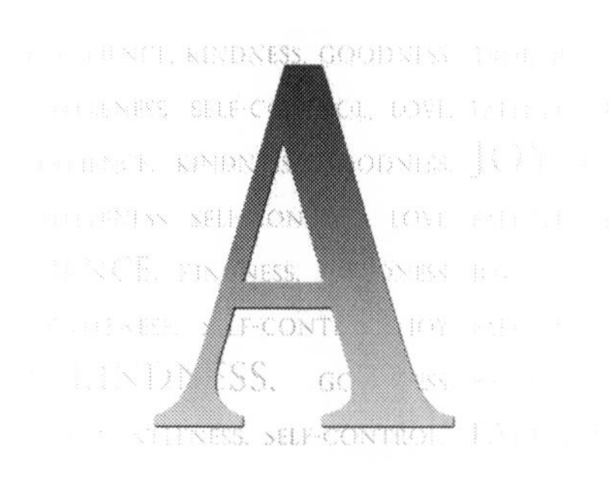

PREFACE & TESTIMONY

As a first-time writer, I would like to share my testimony and give a little background on how this book came to fruition. I am currently thirty-eight years old, and have been a Christian for the last twenty-eight of those years. I am also a wife, mother, registered nurse, and now nurse practitioner. Most importantly, God blessed me with the idea for this book in a dream almost *nine* years ago. *And yes, I am guilty of having a Type A personality!*

Personally, I had always felt that having a Type A personality was a positive quality that I shared with other admirable people, including my parents. We are goal-oriented, task-focused, reliable, detailed, and often competitive. In order to maintain success, I utilized my outgoing Type A personality in every venue throughout the years, including high school, relationships, jobs, college, and even church.

Unfortunately, when trial and tribulation found me in my late twenties, I became acquainted with various negative traits which were hidden inside me: impatience, argumentativeness, and a desire to control, to name a few. Until this age, my life was pretty perfect, and everything went along just as I had planned. I graduated from nursing school, landed a great job as an emergency room nurse, and married a Division I college baseball captain who grew up just twenty minutes from my childhood home. It wasn't until I faced certain trials, which I'll discuss shortly and throughout the book, that I realized my productive Type A characteristics—the ones that granted me success in my life over and over again—were now becoming ineffective. Even worse, it took another five to ten years to realize that my behavior and personality had changed into characteristics that were not becoming of a Christian.

I was always pressed for time due to excessive commitments, and I never delegated because I felt I could do things better myself. Living my life as a busy-body often led to strife within my own family because I missed out on quality time with those I loved the most. For example, I obtained my need for cleanliness from my mother who loves a clean house, but I have often argued that she doesn't know how to sit still and enjoy time with our family because she is constantly cleaning, even before we finish dessert! Also, many Type A personalities can be very controlling and easily angered when things do not go their way. We *never* like to hear that we are wrong—a trait I easily share with my father.

I was, however, blessed with wonderful parents who raised me in church and who always taught me to work hard and enjoy my successes, whether going out to a nice restaurant or on an amazing vacation. They also taught me the value of serving others in a modest way. We are taught in the Bible to perform good works in secret, otherwise God will not reward our service (Matt. 6:1-4). I witnessed my parents provide many services for our family members and neighbors, including mowing yards when they were sick or delivering food when someone had a surgery. These acts of service provided valuable lessons which stressed the importance of showing love and humility to those in need.

This book identifies my own strengths and weaknesses in having a Type A personality and how I utilize it to further my walk with God. So, as you can see from the example of my own life, there are many characteristics and behaviors of a Type A personality that contrast with each other. The Holy Spirit is the only force that can use the good to conquer the bad. And in order to grow, we must recognize our own tribulations, which can easily transform us from within. While we each face different stressors, I invite you to continue reading to learn what trials changed my once *valuable* Type A attributes into *fruitless* traits.

MY STORY

After many years of trying to get pregnant, my husband, Rob, and I were soon diagnosed with unexplained infertility. Patience was *not* a virtue that I possessed when it came to wanting a baby. And pretty soon, my once joyful spirit became frustrated when my prayers continued to go unanswered. After dealing with the thought that I might never become pregnant, I was very angry and quickly started losing my faith in God's plan for our lives. Many times I felt ashamed and embarrassed for being upset with God, and I frequently had to ask forgiveness throughout my years of stress and worry.

Finally, after three years and several failed infertility treatments, we actually conceived naturally and delivered what we thought was a healthy baby girl. While I had a wonderful pregnancy and delivery, we were informed our daughter, Reese, failed her newborn hearing screening. Rob and I were distraught but were quickly told the test had a high rate of false-positives, so Reese was sent for further testing. We had several visits with specialists, and she was later diagnosed with bilateral sensorineural hearing loss. She was quickly fit with pink hearing aids at five months old and began speech therapy at nine months. To this day, we have yet to be given a reason for her hearing loss, which is very troublesome because without an actual cause, her hearing could worsen at any age.

Receiving Reese's diagnosis, and during the events that followed, was only the second time in my life that I felt out of control. We had just been through a very difficult time dealing with infertility only to be handed a new trial, one that our beautiful daughter would also have to bear. After learning of our daughter's hearing loss, the Type A person who lived inside of me wanted to have some type of normal again and educating myself was key in learning how to survive. Obviously, my Type A personality needed to gain some control and I wanted answers. I needed potential causes as well as outcomes for her hearing loss. I was angry at myself. Even as a nurse, I felt completely helpless in that I could do absolutely *nothing* to make it better or change the diagnosis.

I was also unsure of how this disability would affect her in the future. I realized that worrying about Reese's appearance in wearing hearing aids was a minor concern compared to possible functioning deficits. I cried inconsolably once her diagnosis was confirmed. And during all of this, I was also learning how to console my baby as a new mom. Even though I had a great support system, I felt hopeless at times, wondering if all my hopes and dreams for her would ever come true.

As I looked into Reese's eyes, I felt God's overwhelming love in answering my prayer. It was during those times of bonding that I made a commitment to fight with all my heart to ensure Reese received everything she needed to improve any deficits associated with her hearing. Overall, I felt that we coped fairly well due to our Christian faith and the many prayers that were lifted up for all three of us by our family of believers.

Once we adapted to Reese's frequent hearing test schedule, I decided to pursue my nurse practitioner degree and attempt to have a second child. Fortunately, I was able to obtain my master's degree. Regrettably, however, we were unable to conceive a second time. Again I was met with a lack of confidence in God's plan—having one child was not part of *my* plan! Consequently, through impeccable timing, God stepped in to reveal *His* perfect plan.

I was grateful to be chosen as the new women's health nurse practitioner working with my actual gynecologist; however, I was not really sure about working in obstetrics due to my previous infertility experience. I soon discovered my love for talking with pregnant patients and playing with their children as they came to appointments with their mothers. I offered both empathy and sympathy to those dealing with infertility and to women who had delivered babies with unexpected findings. For the first time, I felt that I *could* actually use my former experiences in helping others to not place blame on themselves as I did and to focus on things they could control.

It was at this time that I realized my own failures as a Christian. I learned that during my trials and tribulations of trying to become pregnant, I exhibited a true *lack of faith and obedience* by striving to control my own life and going against God's perfect will. At last, after advising my patients and helping them, I realized that I needed to put my trust back in Him.

THE IDEA

During those early years after Reese was born, I felt I could write to help other Type A mothers through the first stressful months of having a new baby—especially those who were going through similar situations to what my husband and I had faced.

In preparing to write about my experiences and others who were like me, I read many online articles about motherhood in general, as well as specific blogs concerning children affected by hearing loss. I had a wonderful, original idea for a blog titled, *The Type A Mother*, that would focus on coping mechanisms for moms who feel out of control for whatever reason. However, my idea for a small blog totally transformed one night when I had a dream about changing the title to *The Type A Christian.*

The Type A Christian?

What did that even mean?

I toyed with the idea upon waking up and even looked online to see if there were any topics close to that title, and guess what—*nothing.* I think I was actually surprised not to find anything about Christians with Type A personalities. I know God was watching from above laughing as I looked for articles, hashtags, and social media writings. I never really considered writing an actual book. Again, God knew what I was capable of long before I was on board.

After this dream, I attended a women's conference at a local Christian college and was fortunate enough to hear Lisa Harper, a guest speaker from Nashville, in February of 2013. She was amazing! I was enamored by her love for God and was captivated by her testimony. Ms. Harper was a very engaging speaker, and we shared a common affliction as she also desired to become a mother through adoption. During her closing remarks, she asked if any of us felt that God was leading us toward a specific task and requested those individuals to stand up for prayer. I sat in my theater seat that afternoon and watched as many women stood, but I did not. I knew in my heart, however, that God had placed a wonderful idea inside of me; and yet, I still did not rise from my chair.

I felt so guilty over the next few days for not standing. The next Sunday, as my preacher was giving closing remarks, I arose and admitted to my church family that I was ready to stand and work for God on a special project, which He had bestowed upon me. I was reminded of a passage from the Book of Deuteronomy:

> *When you make a vow to the Lord your God, you shall not delay to pay it; for the Lord your God will surely require it of you, and it would be a sin to you. But if you abstain from vowing, it shall not be a sin to you. That which has gone from your lips you shall keep and perform, for you voluntarily vowed to the Lord your God what you have promised with your mouth (23: 21-23).* [1]

As my human side felt weak in my ability to actually write a Christian book, the Holy Spirit within me was definitely rejoicing—as a Type A person, when I make a promise, I intend to keep it! While I felt unworthy to write a *Christian* book, I didn't want to disappoint God because He has never failed in His blessings over me. The more I kept thinking about this idea (which was truly presented as a vision), I finally felt qualified by God to write this book. As a Christian woman who also possesses a raging Type A personality, why wouldn't I fulfill the Lord's work by becoming an author? I have encountered numerous moments while researching and subsequently writing this book when the devil tried to take away my confidence with feelings of inadequacy, but each time I read God's Word and prayed about this project, I immediately felt refreshed.

As I was furthering my knowledge of the Bible, I realized our pastor consistently preached on the fruit of the Spirit in many of his sermons. And I realized that my Type A personality and behavior was not very fruitful at times. In fact, they actually *contradicted* all nine attributes of the fruit of the Spirit altogether.

And *then*, God's revelation for this book started coming together!

I was to discuss how the behaviors of those with Type A personalities conflict with the fruit of the Spirit.

Throughout my research, readings, and actual observations, I have come to realize not everyone who identifies with having a Type A personality exhibits *all* the negative traits, including myself. I wanted this book to identify both the positive and negative behaviors of Type A. If we are able to identify our inconsiderate conduct, we can then learn how to improve the relationships we have with both Christians and non-Christians. As we successfully transform our personalities to that of our Creator, we will not only develop but also mature our fruit. In fact, one admirable characteristic of a Type A believer is to be goal-oriented. Can you imagine the success of a believer whose goal is to further the Kingdom of God?

I fully hope you enjoy the information in this book. I have worked diligently to ensure God's Word is exercised appropriately and will benefit each of us as we learn how to best utilize our Type A traits.

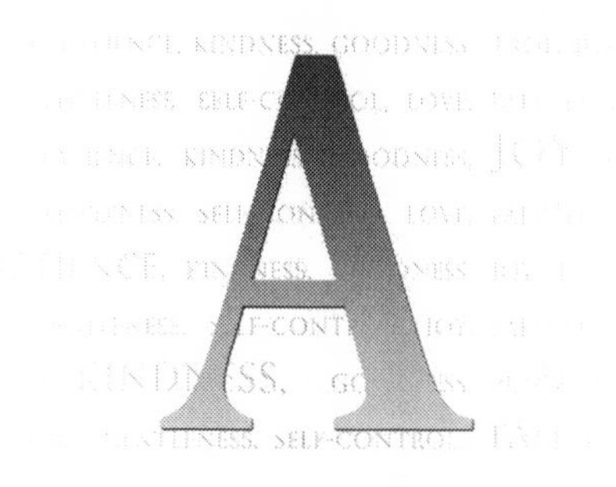

INTRODUCTION

Have you ever credited your success to having a Type A personality? If so, then you join an overwhelming number of people in the world who consider themselves Type A. There are various Type A qualities, and just like other personality types, some qualities are positive and some are negative. While many of our successes are driven by our beneficial traits, we unfortunately utilize some not-so-favorable traits in order to meet our goals.

So then, what is a *Type A Christian*? It is someone who has learned how to use their positive personality traits and has overcome negative behaviors in order to fulfill their role as a follower of Christ.

The overall objective for this book is to help you employ self-examination of your personality and to determine if your behaviors coincide with the fruit of the Spirit that we as Christians are called to display. Regardless of personality type, you will learn which traits to *grow* and which to *prune*.

Adverse behavior patterns identified with Type A personalities undeniably conflict with the fruit of the Spirit. What if you realize, through the course of this book, that your various Type A behaviors do not coincide with Christian principles taught in the Bible? While many Type A traits are considered positive and essential to a productive life, most of our controlling behaviors are *not* consistent with the Holy Spirit who lives inside of us. Together, we can learn how to overcome these negative traits to best benefit the Church as we strive to spread the Gospel.

In this book, you will first learn about the different personality types and behaviors based upon various psychologists throughout history.

Next, you will take a one-of-a-kind personality quiz to assess common behaviors regarding your Christian conduct, which may identify unfavorable habits.

Later in the book, we will discuss which Type A traits to improve and which ones need to be transformed altogether.

Each chapter in this book reveals valuable information that will impact your walk with Christ and the furthering of His Kingdom. God made us all unique and granted us with varying personalities to fulfill His purpose, but we need to ensure the world doesn't completely eliminate our ability to produce good fruit.

While we, the Type A Christians of this world, generously declare our love for God, sometimes we lose agape, or selfless love, for our fellow brothers and sisters in Christ. While we usually anticipate accolades for our services, we exhibit certain actions and behaviors which can adversely impact our ability to witness and decrease our opportunities to lead others to Christ.

As a general population, we are overworked, overscheduled, overcommitted, and over-exhausted! As a women's health care provider, I have observed individuals facing various yet similar stressors such as tensions within the family, school, work, finances, social obligations, and even church. Our stressors are mostly related to our perceptions in reaching success at much younger ages.

Being a nurse (now a practitioner), I have been blessed to devote the last seventeen years of my life to serving others. However, during most of those years, when my shift would end for the day, I was a different person than when I was on the clock. I focused on myself and aspects of my life that were not going as planned. During my time away from work, I was not attentive to the needs of others, which often affected the ones I loved the most.

After realizing my lack of faith in dealing with infertility, and even now in trying to understand why our daughter has a lifelong impairment, I started to understand that my previous, respectable Type A traits had weakened into the opposites of my Christian fruit.

I also realized the world teaches the need for *"things"* such as large homes, fancy cars, and designer clothes to feel accepted and happy rather than finding joy in the Lord and being filled with the Holy Spirit.

If our fruit benefits others rather than ourselves, then we will be blessed in all areas of our lives. Learning to improve yourself as a Type A Christian will be a tedious process, but God will utilize your invaluable personality traits to further His Kingdom, just like He is using me in writing this book!

When God provides opportunities to display our fruit for others, we must never shy away from using our abilities to do the will of our Creator. Submitting to authority can be difficult for many, but especially for those of us who are Type A—mostly because we never like being told what to do. However, when we submit to God and the Holy Spirit, our lives will be richly blessed.

Can you imagine the possibilities if Type A Christians utilized only the good attributes during their Christian walk? How successful could your Christian walk be in bringing others to Christ? The Bible describes the word success in other terms, such as victory and triumph. Think about the many victories and triumphs you could achieve by utilizing your best personality features. Now that's a victorious Type A Christian!

The principles learned in this book can also bring success to the church as a whole. For example, after discussing the idea for my book with my current pastor, he loved the idea so much he enlisted four other *"Type A Christians"* to create a new committee to improve planning and preparation for various church events. For those with Type A tendencies, we often think five minutes, five hours, and even five months ahead of others, which makes us successful in maintaining organization for any church. Our new Type A committee has been a wonderful addition because, in our preacher's words, *"Things get done!"* Our pastor can fully rely on our committee to carry out our tasks in planning and can rest easy knowing every detail has been acknowledged—sometimes twice! Having a specific schedule for church events and missions will also benefit both Type A and non-Type A congregation members as well as non-believers.

Now, here's the best part. By improving our strengths as Type A Christians, not only will we improve relationships with others around us but also in our relationship with God. As we seek ways to serve others, we are promised many rewards from our Father in Heaven. Believers are already promised an eternal home with our Heavenly Father, but if we choose to submit to the Holy Spirit, Jesus *will* reward us for displaying our fruit in our many acts of service. Imagine Jesus saying to you, *"Well done, my faithful servant,"* and knowing you took full advantage of *all* your opportunities in furthering His Church.

God made us all unique and granted us with varying identities to fulfill His purpose, but we need to ensure our personalities do not completely weaken our ability to produce good fruit. So, how do we transform ourselves—turning the negative traits into positive virtues? Well, that's the purpose of this book. Inspired by God, I hope this text will give an optimistic outlook on how we can embrace the traits we have and how to improve those we desperately need to alter. I hope the verses used within this book enhance your understanding and spur a movement within each of us to become consistent readers of the Word, better developers of our fruit, and even better followers of God.

Let's find out if *you've* got what it takes to be a *Type A Christian*!

CHAPTER ONE
PERSONALITY TYPES

A quote from French novelist Jean-Baptiste Alphonse Karr states that *"every man has three characters—that which he exhibits, that which he has, and that which he thinks he has."*[2] While Karr wrote this during the 1800s, his statement could not be more perfect for today's society, especially with the increasing popularity of social media. Furthermore, his actual quote was similar to the apostle Paul from the New Testament. Paul realized the power that sin has over our lives when he acknowledged the fruit he *wanted* to display, but was unable to fulfill while in the flesh. He later admitted how sin caused variations in his spiritual character and led him to practice fruitless traits (Romans 7:15-20).

In this first chapter, we will look at the history of personality and various personality types as well as the extreme differences between the fruit of the Spirit as compared to less than desirable Type A traits. While our personalities are unique just as God intended, we must utilize them appropriately without allowing sin to overcome us. In order to maintain our Christian behaviors, we must prevent sin from altering our personalities for the purpose of pleasing others.

Despite variations in our skill levels and talents, we all want to be our best whether at home, work, school, or church. Unfortunately, life happens and sometimes we are met with circumstances we cannot always change. These events, no matter the age of occurrence, may lead to specific changes within us—emotionally, physically, and spiritually. Perhaps a child who was neglected grows up to have trust issues or a young girl who was raped suffers intimacy issues with her future spouse. Life events, whether positive or negative, greatly impact who we become as individuals and greatly affect our personalities and behaviors.

While some are fortunate enough to be raised by Christian parents and saved at an early age, it is essential to realize not everyone is privileged to live the same life. Hence, showing love and compassion rather than mocking or judging others with different backgrounds is a necessity. We all face issues within our lives that we wish we could change, and thankfully, there is One who *wants* to shape and mold us so we can prosper. We will never be perfect, but we are made perfect in the love of our Heavenly Father (I John 4:17).

Thankfully, God has made us in His image but also created us to be unique in our own ways. We all have special talents that God has instilled in each of us. All we have to do to receive the blessing of the Holy Spirit is accept His Son. It is the

Holy Spirit that will help us carry out our gifts. These gifts, or attributes, are not only a blessing from God but also a blessing when we take advantage of opportunities to share His love with others.

UNDERSTANDING PERSONALITY

So what is personality? In both Greek and Latin, the word stems from the root word *"persona,"* which represents the word *"mask."* The definition states that personality is *"the combination of characteristics or qualities that form an individual's distinctive character"* or *"the sum total of all the behavioural [sic] and mental characteristics by means of which an individual is recognized as being unique."*[3] It is further clarified as patterns in thinking, feeling, and behaving. Synonyms for personality include temperament, persona, disposition, nature, and behavior.

Personality and behavior have both been subjects of study for many centuries, even before Jesus lived on earth. The Ancient Greek *"Father of Medicine,"* otherwise known as Hippocrates, was one of the first to study the human body in regards to personality. His *"Humors Theory"* suggested that personality was based upon physiologic components within the body, specifically four body fluids or humors—blood, yellow bile, black bile, and phlegm.[4] It wasn't until 1879 that a German physiologist, Wilhelm Wundt, actually looked at the human body and personality as two separate entities. He was later given the title as the first *"Father of Psychology"* as he objectively monitored individuals in three areas, including thoughts, images, and feelings.[5] He also believed that most individuals utilized two or more temperaments within their personality traits.[6]

The twentieth century led to the development of personality tests by well-known psychologists, including Carl Jung and Sigmund Freud. While Jung may not be as well-known as Freud, it was actually Jung who coined the *"two major attitudes or orientations of personality—extroversion and introversion. He also identified four basic functions (thinking, feeling, sensing, and intuiting), which in a cross-classification yield eight pure personality types."*[7] The aforementioned functions have been used in many personality tests and quizzes since his time.

The Viennese neuropathologist, Freud, utilized psychoanalysis in his attempt to treat his patients by allowing them to speak freely in describing their thoughts. He later utilized the depiction of an iceberg to describe the three levels of the mind. The iceberg viewed atop the surface of the water was described as the *conscious* mind, the iceberg at water level is described as the *preconscious*, while the iceberg below the surface was the *unconscious* mind, which Freud described as the major source of our behavior with the largest size or depth.[8]

Freud was also the creator of the infamous terms ego and superego, and liked to define the meaning of dreams. (I believe that interpretation of dreams was utilized well before Freud, just look in the Old Testament—particularly with Joseph and Daniel.) Moreover, Jung and Freud both believed that an individual's personality and behavior was based upon previous experiences, but Jung also believed people are shaped by their future goals as well.[9]

In the late 1950s, Erik Erikson developed the theory of psychosocial development which identified eight stages from infant to adulthood. This theory focused on how one's personality was affected by various outcomes, both positive and negative. Erikson also proposed that personality development continued to occur throughout one's life based upon experiences within the various stages.[10] He stressed the importance of the adolescent time period as *"it was a crucial stage for developing a person's identity."*[11] Erikson believed that as a person accomplished each stage, they would gain virtues, including hope, will, purpose, competency, fidelity, love, care, and wisdom.[12]

For example, the first stage, *Trust versus Mistrust*, occurs at infancy, as stated by Erikson. An infant may successfully proceed to the second stage with loving and providing parents who offer round-the-clock care, including feedings, changings, and adequate interaction. These actions would later indicate *trust* on the infant's part, as well as the virtue of *Hope* as the infant ages to the next stage and feels secure in a safe and loving support system. However, if the infant does *not* have adequate caretakers, then *mistrust* is present and *fear* develops as the infant ages.

The most important stage believed by Erikson is the adolescent stage, and is titled *Ego Identity versus Role Confusion*. This stage occurs between the ages of 12-18. The goal here is to move successfully through this phase in order to obtain the virtue of *Fidelity*. Many parents understand the time we have with our children is very limited. As babies, it seems they will never grow up, but once children start middle school, the time we have with them is over in the blink of an eye.

This stage is marked when a teenager says goodbye to being a child and tries to find a sense of self and identity as he or she matures into an adult both mentally and physically. They actively try to see where they fit in with others, whether in school, sports, clubs, or other activities. Once they have the confidence that is born from a stable and supportive family, they can secure Fidelity. *"Fidelity involves being able to commit oneself to others on the basis of accepting others, even when there may be ideological differences,"* which is demonstrated through faithfulness, loyalty, and support.[13] However, if the adolescent is never offered expectations about his or her future goals or aspirations, they may be confused (i.e. role confusion) and develop poor self-esteem. Furthermore, if being a contributing member of society is not portrayed in the child's home by the parents, then it is probably not going to be a priority to the teenager. When the teenager seeks to explore where he or she fits in, they may be apathetic to others who may be a source of support or encouragement, like teachers, coaches, or those within the church family they have been part of. This may lead to identity crisis and possible rebellion if pressured by others and may cause symptoms of depression.[14]

I remember listening to a guest speaker in high school who spoke about his young grandchild. He was constantly asking the boy what he wanted to be when he grew up. Obviously, when his grandson was younger, he picked the most exciting and dangerous, yet pleasurable job he could think of—a trash truck operator! While this is an important job, and I am very grateful for our local employees, this guest speaker knew the importance of establishing life goals and instilling this in his grandchild at an early age without applying pressure.

My own daughter, who is currently in the fourth grade, has had many occupational aspirations including becoming a lyricist, drummer, guitarist, actress, gymnast, race car driver, ice skater, chef, and most recently, a bakery owner. She even told my mother-in-law after baking a cake that she didn't need to help clean the dishes because she would have *"employees"* to wash pans at her bakery. So, even though Reese may be more in tune with her future than others, I still want her to dream big while including God in all of her planning—and yes, she is learning how to wash dishes!

I do agree with Erikson when he said that we face many stages in our lives. I have evidenced others who have been successful and others who have not—all based on individual choices. I stress to my daughter the importance of making the right choices throughout her life, even when she may be the only one, not because I said so, but because it is what *God* says. If we trust in the Lord with all our hearts and stay within His purpose, He will direct our paths and lead us to a full life (Proverbs 3:5-6)—not a life without trials, but a full life because we serve the Living God.

While Freud's and Erikson's theories are more well-known, Freud's theories were never really shown to predict future behavior quite as well as Jung's theories.[15] In fact, Jung's theories are still utilized in one of the most commonly used personality tests, *The Myers-Briggs Type Indicator*, which was developed in the '40s and '50s and first used in 1962.[16] There are ninety-three yes/no questions, which can help determine one's specific personality based on sixteen different types. This personality quiz was developed by a mother and her daughter, Katherine Cook-Briggs and Isabel Briggs-Myers, to look at various traits, including extroversion versus introversion, sensing versus intuition, thinking versus feeling, and judging versus perception. There are many combinations based upon these characteristics, which can lead to sixteen different types as mentioned above.

A quote by Briggs-Myers states that *"good type development can be achieved at any age by anyone who cares to understand his or her own gifts and the appropriate use of those gifts."*[17] I find this statement interesting as Briggs-Myers obtained much of her data collection from those pursuing careers in the nursing and medical fields. While devoting twenty-five years to analyzing physicians and nurses, she felt it was necessary for these students to determine their personality type to see if they were well-suited for such careers as they held *"others' lives in their hands."*[18] Her quote is equally important for our spiritual gifts and fruit because we as Christians can also make a difference in the lives of others. Our message of hope and expression of grace to those who are lost not only fulfills the Great Commission but also furthers God's eternal Kingdom.

As previously defined, our personalities may also be explained via genetic disposition passed down from former generations or based upon the role of a given environment, such as parenting styles and cultural expectations.[19] One author writes that personalities are based upon both thought and emotion as well as consistency in behaviors, biological needs, awareness and responses, and how we interact with others.[20] While God created our physical features to be diverse, our underlying personalities are equally unique. As we grow and mature, we learn to identify and accept who we are as individuals and hopefully understand who God wants us to be for His purpose.

Our personalities are vital in how we connect to the world around us. So it is imperative to our purpose that we remain faithful in sharing the Gospel and teaching others about Christ.

TYPE A PERSONALITY: TO HAVE OR NOT TO HAVE?

Now that we have a little understanding of the history of personality and type, let's discover when *Type A personality* became a household name. The phenomenon known as Type A was first identified by two San Francisco cardiologists, Dr. Meyer Friedman and Dr. Ray Rosenman. Along with their secretary, they observed specific behaviors in their office waiting room by some of their male patients and later monitored the men's responses in stressful situations. They discovered some of the men displayed a sense of urgency and impatience, as well as a competitive, self-critical persona. These men also viewed other individuals in negative ways and were often hostile and angry toward others. The cardiologists determined their patients with aggressive behavior were more at risk for stress-related illnesses such as high blood pressure.

Based on their questionnaire and research in 1976, male participants aged 39-59 responded to questions including (1) feelings of guilt when using time to relax, (2) if joy resulted only from winning, (3) the pace at which individuals live (move/eat/walk), and (4) how often one completes more than one task simultaneously (i.e. multi-tasker).[21] Based on the individuals' responses, they were identified as either *"overt behavior pattern A,"* which consisted mostly of *"time urgency and hostility,"* while participants who were more relaxed and less anxious were considered *"overt behavior pattern B."*[22] The personality labels were later simplified to Type A and Type B.[23] Following eight and a half years of study, men classified with Type A personalities were more at risk for cardiovascular or coronary heart disease than Type B males involved in the research.[24] The cardiologists later published a New York Times bestseller titled, *Type A Behavior and Your Heart.*[25] Subsequently, *Type A* became a household name.

It's interesting to note that Type A and Type B personalities have only been defined in the last thirty to forty years, despite their trademark characteristics. So what are the differences between Type A and B personalities? Type B's are typically more relaxed, and although they are still competitive, they tend *not* to focus on a sense of urgency as compared to those with Type A personalities. On the other hand, they may procrastinate and work at their own pace, while finding enjoyment in their successes rather than quickly moving to the next goal similar to someone with Type A. Type B's are usually more tolerant than individuals with Type A, thus they have decreased levels of anxiety.[26]

Along with these common personality types, there are two other personalities described as Type C and Type D, which are based on distinctive behaviors. Type C individuals tend to be followers, but as you can imagine they may also lead a life of regret as they tend to let others lead their path instead of being more assertive in their own choices.[27] *"Pushover"* is one word used to describe a Type C as they often choose silence to avoid conflict and to appease their friends or co-workers. Unfortunately, individuals with Type C still maintain feelings of resentment and possibly anger, which may be even more damaging to their personality because they are not being true to their own ideas and goals. While they often focus on details, they may face depression because they lack boldness and allowing others to persuade them.[28]

On the other hand, Type D actually stands for *"distressed"* and is characterized by individuals who are typically pessimistic—someone those of us in the South call a *"Negative Nelly."* I once heard Dr. David Jeremiah on one of his *Turning Point* radio broadcasts describe this type of Christian personality as someone who may have been baptized in *prune juice*! No one likes to be around someone who is negative and complains all the time without offering suggestions or ideas for improvements. A particular event may occur and go unnoticed by a Type B, yet may cause a ruined day for a Type D.[29] They typically live a life of fear and isolation, which can lead to depression[30] as well as other stress-related illnesses and coronary heart disease similar to Type A.[31]

Obviously, we all have various characteristic traits that we utilize throughout our lives—making conscious decisions in our reactions to everyday events. Limiting ourselves to just one type is preposterous; however, in general terms, we can each categorize ourselves and those closest to us pretty easily.

There were obvious questions in relation to Dr. Friedman's and Dr. Rosenman's study. Most importantly, what about the female population and their risks? This was addressed in several later studies. Women who were classified as having Type A personalities did not show the same increased risk for disease, perhaps due to improved 'coping strategies' than that of males."[32] It was also noted in the 1980s that hostility was the primary trait that led to cardiovascular illness.[33]

A later study in 2012 actually confirmed that one-third of all individuals with Type A did in fact have cardiovascular disorders over other health-related illnesses.[34] In fact, this study also showed that patients with cardiac disorders typically suffered increased levels of anxiety than that of non-cardiac patients.[35] It also stated that those with Type A behavior patterns worried *less* about their health, which led patients to *"underestimate the need to modify unhealthy lifestyles."*[36]

Why do Type A's not worry about their health as much? This is most likely a result of their chosen priorities on seemingly more important items—*things they can control.* Cardiologists currently preach lifestyle modifications to their patients, yet they do not understand *why* their patients have trouble adhering to the changes. Most cardiac patients with true Type A behavior do not feel they will suffer consequences from their actions, whether it is from eating a terrible diet or lack of exercise.[37]

Is this not the same for us as Christians with Type A personalities? We must learn in our Christian walk that our actions *do* in fact carry consequences, sometimes positive, sometimes negative, sometimes short-lived, sometimes for an entire lifetime. Just as cardiac patients who are Type A will eventually feel the physical consequences of their actions, good or bad, so we too as Christians will experience the spiritual consequences of our Type A actions.

A NEW PHENOMENON

As mentioned previously, we are constantly learning about ourselves throughout our lives based on experiences—both good and bad. So why is it considered a benefit to hire someone who is more Type A than Type B? When did Type A go from a negative behavior pattern to an admirable personality? Do we compromise our Christian virtues to fulfill our goals? Do we find ourselves competing against others just to prove we can win and achieve personal recognition? Then why would we as Christians *want* to portray ourselves as hostile Type A individuals? It is interesting to note that Dr. Friedman once called himself a *"recovering Type A."*[38]

Unfortunately, we live in a fast-paced world with a sink-or-swim mentality toward life in general. We all want to see ourselves as the best we can be, and for some, this means stepping on others to get to the top. We use any means to further ourselves or to rise above others, including money, our children, and fictitious stories. We want others to see that we can be the perfect spouse, homeroom parent, baker, painter, gardener, and yes, even Christian.

Type A behavior has taken on a completely new meaning from when it was first studied in regard to adverse health effects and negative personality characteristics. We are so concerned with setting an ideal standard for others that we are easily blinded by the negative examples we are portraying in our daily lives. Nonetheless, as Christians, we must be willing examples for others and not for dishonest gain (I Peter 5:2). We must humble ourselves unto God *"that He may exalt [us] in due time"* (I Peter 5:6). In any environment or situation, we must remain close to our Creator and pray for wisdom rather than resorting to typical Type A characteristics and traits devoid of the Holy Spirit.

So what are typical Type A characteristics? You might be surprised. Here is a list of notorious Type A Traits:

Easily angered, aggressive, multi-tasker, goal-oriented without appreciating rewards, hostile, quick-tempered, easily irritated, desires recognition, poor team player, arrogant, sense of urgency, lack of compassion, frequently interrupts, self-critical, self-reliant, competitive, over-reacts, impatient, high-work involvement, dislikes delays, views the worst in others, bullying behavior, and inability to rest.

The Diagnostic Criteria Psychosomatic Research, or DCPR, first recognized patients with Type A Behavior as a syndrome in 1995 based on validated interviews utilizing Friedman and Rosenman's original research.[39] "According to the DCPR criteria, Type A behaviour [sic] refers to the presence of at least five of nine characteristics:

> *"(i) excessive degree of involvement in work and other activities subject to deadlines; (ii) steady and pervasive sense of time urgency; (iii) display of motor-expressive features (rapid and explosive speech, abrupt body movements, tensing of facial muscles, hand gestures) indicating sense of being under the pressure of time; (iv) hostility and cynicism; (v) irritable mood; (vi) tendency to speed up physical activities; (vii) tendency to speed up mental activities; (viii) high intensity of desire for achievement and recognition and (ix) high competitiveness."*[40]

How do you stack up to the traits and characteristics listed above? As I mentioned previously, I once believed having Type A traits were considered beneficial; however, as many commentaries illustrate, individuals with Type A do not always put forth encouraging fruit. We all face trials within our lives, but it is important to read our Bible and learn that with trials come the promise of success from our Father (I Samuel 18:14).

I can unfortunately admit to at least *five* of the nine characteristics. And, you know what? I previously considered most of these traits as admirable. But why do individuals have such a desire to proudly boast their Type A image? Why did *I* once think these traits were positive—for excelling in school or in my career? What about my family, my church, or my witnessing ability? Do I want to hurry and rush through time spent with my family and God? What about non-believers—do we *choose* to hurry through an opportunity with an individual because we place higher importance on other people or events based on personal agendas? How would you feel knowing you could be the difference in someone going to Heaven or Hell?

It is imperative we understand who we are, but we also need to learn why God gave us specific Type A traits and characteristics—I do believe there are many benefits. Just as the former physician who identified himself as a *recovering* Type A, he recognized the negative aspects associated with these traits and developed a desire to change.

So why is it important to relate this prevalent behavior pattern to the fruit of the Spirit?

Were *any* of the attributes listed in the above traits—*love, joy, peace, longsuffering/patience, kindness, goodness, faithfulness, gentleness/meekness, and self-control*? (Galatians 5:22-23.) No, of course not!

None of the traits listed above are synonymous with Paul's written attributes to the churches of Galatia on the blessings of receiving the Holy Spirit. Let's take a look at the following chart to see how they compare and contrast:

FRUIT	**TYPE A TRAITS**
1. Love	1. Easily Angered
2. Joy	2. Over-burdened
3. Peace	3. Aggressive
4. Patience	4. Sense of Urgency
5. Kindness	5. Inconsiderate
6. Goodness	6. Self-centered
7. Meekness	7. Proud
8. Faithfulness	8. Self-reliant
9. Self-control	9. Impulsive

As previously mentioned in Erikson's stages of progression, if we as Christians learn to walk in the Spirit (Galatians 5:16), we can successfully gain these nine virtues, or fruit, as the apostle Paul prefers to call them. *These* are the true qualities that I want to acquire in order to successfully equip myself as a Christian and to bless others.

Now that we understand basic developmental theories and assorted personality types in relation to the fruit of the Spirit, it is time to explore your own personality type. The next chapter provides a personality quiz that you have *never* taken before. This quiz will help determine your primary personality behaviors within your Christian walk in as little as nine questions. We will also discuss various modifications regarding personality types, which are essential in maturing our fruit.

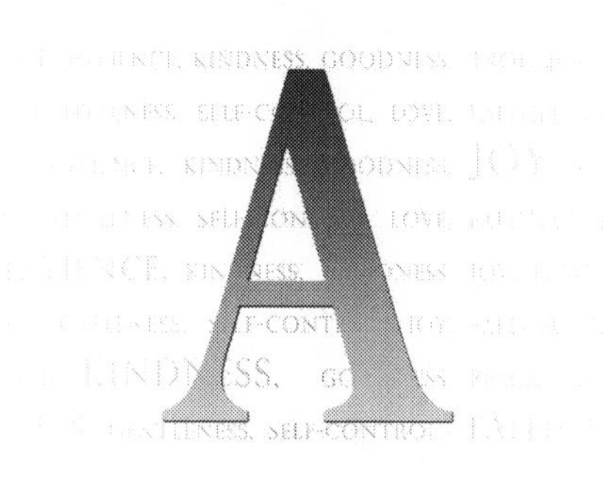

CHAPTER TWO
PERSONALITY QUIZ

When researching personality tests, I was totally overwhelmed at the various quizzes available online. Some identify our likeness to superheroes, animals, and even celebrities, while the more common quizzes help determine strengths and weaknesses, careers that best suit an individual's skills, and even compatibility quizzes for finding a soul mate. The one common goal with each of these tests is to gain further knowledge about oneself. This chapter provides a one-of-a-kind personality quiz based on the *behaviors* of a believer. It will clarify the characteristics we typically portray rather than the fruit we choose to display to those we encounter. This quiz is different because it is specific to believers in the church setting. For if we treat our brothers and sisters in Christ with contempt, then how will we ever learn how to treat non-believers?

Prior to the questionnaire to determine those who were Type A, the first personality test ever recorded was actually identified as the Woodworth's Personal Data Sheet in 1917. This survey assessed United States Army soldiers at risk of "shell shock" if captured during World War I. Since that time, there have been many personality tests throughout history, including inkblot tests, psychological assessments, subjective interviews, objective questionnaires, self-response tests, and now smart phone apps for quick personality evaluations—which is great for the Type A person who is *always* on the go.

Personality tests are still a popular phenomenon. The Myers-Briggs Type Test mentioned in the last chapter is utilized by an estimated four million people yearly. It catapulted personality testing into a $4 billion profitable industry.[41]

We are all created in the image of our Father in Heaven—no matter the gender, color, race, or even personality. And just as Briggs-Myers was impartial towards others with different personalities, she was *"always appreciative and interested, [but] never critical."*[42] This is what we need to understand regarding the society in which we live today. We will always face people with different temperaments and behaviors—some are learned and some are mechanisms used for survival. We should fulfill the work as directed in the Bible and love one another as well as appreciate our differences. But we must *start* with our brothers and sisters in Christ and *then* carry over into our mission of evangelism. We must grow together and focus on the same goals before we can be influential to our families and followed by our communities.

Now, I'm not implying there were never any arguments between the disciples. They even argued about which of them was the greatest. Seriously, they were *not* God in the flesh; they were real men born of flesh into sin. If they did not fully believe their purpose was to spread the love of God to all men and women as well as proclaim Jesus as the Resurrected Messiah, they would not have focused their entire lives on spreading the Good News.

Yet, we as Christians have a difficult time showing our love for God. Most of us do not bow our heads for ten seconds to pray during lunch in front of co-workers. When we don't have time in our busy schedules to stop and talk, we often glance away when someone comes toward us. Sometimes our negative behaviors can be very discouraging through both spoken and unspoken communication. It's time for us to realize our actions play a huge role in leading others to Christ. Consequently, the *lack* of actions may lead to an eternity of suffering souls.

Most Type A quizzes include questions regarding sense of urgency, competitive nature, or personal achievement goals, but I wanted this quiz to be different than any personality test you have ever taken. This one-of-a-kind personality quiz will help you dig deep into your own personality and your own Christian walk.

I actually completed this quiz after writing the rest of the book. I felt such a strong presence of God throughout the process of writing, but I wasn't sure how the personality test would come together, so I left it to the end. Finally, one beautiful, fall day, I sat down and prayed as I usually do prior to writing, and the quiz began to naturally spill onto paper. I completed *all* of my questions and answers in one day.

I decided to use possible examples and experiences within the church or the Christian community that may lead to strife within our family of believers rather than our everyday world. My reasoning—if we cannot improve our relationships with fellow believers, then how will we ever cultivate our behaviors for the purpose of sharing the Good News with non-Christians?

Disclaimer: There are no right or wrong answers within this quiz. Hopefully, this will help you realize areas of concern in your own walk, just as I have. Whatever the answer, this is a time of reflection to better improve production, growth, and maintenance of our fruit. Remember, while our actions do not always correlate with our intentions, others may be quick to judge our negative conduct, but God looks at our hearts and continues to love us (I Samuel 16:7).

Go to the following link to download the
quiz if you prefer to print and answer:

www.chasingkitespublishing.com/authors/autumn-hoover

PERSONALITY TYPE QUIZ

1. Your husband is preparing to serve the weekly church communion when an unknown guest sitting beside you asks, *"how often does the church take communion"*—you quickly answer, *"weekly"*—but, the guest informs you that she does not feel communion should be done that frequently as it loses its importance. Which one of the following would you most likely say in response:

A. *"Communion is part of worship and it is very important to stay on a schedule."* (spoken very aggressively toward the guest)

B. *"I've never really thought about it; it's just something I've grown accustomed to each week."*

C. *"I was always used to quarterly communion at my other church; I guess you're right."*

D. *"No one in the church listens to anyone's opinions and everyone does whatever they want."*

E. *"I agree with the decisions of the elders within my church in holding a weekly communion and would be happy to discuss Scripture following the service to indicate the basis and importance for their decision in having a weekly communion."*

2. Your church is hosting a guest speaker who you have looked forward to hearing speak over the last few months. Unfortunately, the speaker had a change in his schedule, and you just realized he is preaching on the same day you have nursery duty. Which one of the following actions would you most likely take:

A. You quickly walk to the nursery avoiding others who say *"hello,"* pace the floors in the nursery while holding a crying infant, and overreact to the other volunteer worker after she informed you of your mistake in using a wrong diaper.

B. You tell your spouse to take good notes to determine if the speaker was worth the excitement as you head off to the nursery to play with the new toddlers.

C. You really want to ask another church member to trade nursery rotations with you, but you are too afraid they will say *"No,"* so you do not ask.

D. You loudly and hastily complain to the nursery director about serving in the nursery as it is a waste of your time and the room smells like dirty diapers.

E. You ask a member of the media staff to record the message as you continue serving in the nursery and fulfill your commitment.

3. At the end of church service, the children's minister expresses his gratitude to the church for graciously budgeting a portion of funding toward a youth conference. He feels this will be a great outreach for the community and cannot wait to invite the teens in the surrounding areas. You currently do not have any children in the youth group. Which of the following would be your response:

A. You become very hostile when you learn the church is not funding any trips for younger children and decide to approach fellow church members on the financial committee to question their decisions.

B. After the children's minister offers a word of thanks, you look at your weekly church bulletin to check upcoming events for younger children.

C. After listening to the children's minister, you reach for your checkbook to write a special offering specifically for the youth conference; however, you change your mind when your spouse advises against giving an offering to groups in the church which don't involve your children.

D. You think it's ridiculous to send youth on an overnight trip when they could learn at church for free.

E. You fondly remember all the youth trips you attended and how your Christian walk was strengthened, and you decide to pledge a special offering specifically for this youth conference. You later ask the children's minister for ways to volunteer in preparation for the upcoming conference.

4. Your church has experienced wonderful growth within the youth group, and the leadership team has recommended the addition of a gymnasium to accommodate the increase. However, after various research, the leadership team votes against the addition at this time. Which one of the following identifies how you would react:

A. While you tried to be patient with the leadership team as they came to a conclusion, you quickly become angry as you do not agree with their decision and fear the church will not continue to grow.

B. You are glad the leadership team finally came to a decision, but it didn't matter as you do not have any children who could benefit from having a gym.

C. While you believed the church had potential, you are frustrated that the leadership team never asked for ideas regarding other areas for improvement.

D. You quickly complain to the leadership team and preacher that your current church is too small and growth will soon stop. In fact, you are thinking of leaving to find a new church.

E. While a gymnasium addition may offer opportunities, you embrace the current decision made by the leadership team and offer your help to improve the current church in order to maintain and promote growth.

5. Your preacher had unexpected surgery, and while his wife is still able to prepare meals for him, the leader of the food team encourages various teams to take three meals rather than the one meal that is typically taken to families in need within the church. You respond in the following way:

A. You are upset by having to cook another meal as this week is terribly busy at work, but in order to outdo others on the food teams, you know you have to cook your best dish and you do not ask your spouse to help because you cook better by yourself.

B. You kindly agree to cook a dish but probably cannot have it ready for a few days.

C. You quickly become frustrated and angry and think to yourself how ridiculous it is to treat the pastor any different, but you decide to sign up to bring the extra meal anyway.

D. You complain to the leader of the food team and ask why we should treat the preacher any differently.

E. You realize that your preacher is literally on-call for every member of the congregation including weekends and holidays, and you gladly request to bring his favorite dish to show your appreciation to him and his family for their service to the church.

6. You helped organize a clean-up day at the church and made appropriate lists for all the tasks that need to be completed. The pastor wants to show his appreciation by supplying lunch to all those participating in the clean-up; however, lunch arrived before all the tasks were completed and everyone stopped cleaning to eat. Which reaction would you probably have in this situation:

A. You realize you have 30 minutes of work left and are already scheduled to meet friends for coffee, so you offer a quick "thank you" to the preacher but continue working to complete your tasks.

B. Even though you have 30 minutes of work left, you are excited to eat your favorite pizza and decide to finish your tasks after lunch.

C. You realize you only have 30 minutes to clean and try to continue, but the preacher tells you that the church looks great and to finish at the next scheduled clean-up, so you stop cleaning to eat against your preference to keep working.

D. In front of the preacher, you walk into the kitchen and tell everyone to finish cleaning before eating. Besides, you don't like that cheap pizza anyway.

E. You decide to take a time-out to eat lunch, and commend the preacher as well as the church volunteers regarding their desire to serve.

7. An evening church service is devoted to other believers offering their personal testimonies and the importance of maintaining a Christian life. One of the church members later admits to using drugs in her past life before becoming a Christian—a fact you did not realize. Which response is in line with how you would react:

A. On the car ride home, your husband shares his admiration for her testimony, but you, on the other hand, just don't understand how people can make such bad decisions and remark that they should learn to make better choices.

B. You were deeply moved by her testimony and look forward to the next speaker.

C. You were totally captivated by her testimony until your friend walks by and whispers to you not to invite her to the next small group meeting for fear of being associated with her former lifestyle, and you reluctantly agree.

D. You are completely blindsided by the fact that the church would let a former drug-addict speak in front of the congregation and plan to inform the preacher of your utter disappointment after the service.

E. You quickly find the woman who offered her testimony and express your gratitude and appreciation for her humility, integrity, and desire to speak. You then share what obstacle God helped you overcome in your life before accepting Christ and how humbled you felt when other Christians embraced you into their family of believers.

8. During an open church prayer request time, a young married couple requests prayer to become pregnant after two unsuccessful years of trying. They do not wish to see a fertility specialist as they are fully trusting and reliant on God's ability to help them conceive. You respond with which of the following:

A. You quickly find your way to the couple and advise they have waited too long without seeing a professional, and you would be happy to contact the fertility specialist who evaluated one of your friends and try to get them an appointment as soon as possible.

B. You find the couple after church and wish them well with becoming pregnant.

C. You sadly remember the difficult time in becoming pregnant yourself and think about giving the young couple your contact information, but you are not ready to discuss your past medical information, even though it could prove beneficial.

D You quickly walk up to the couple and loudly ask in front of other members of the congregation if it is the wife's or the husband's fault for not being able to conceive?

E. You take a moment and write down the young couple's name to remember during your personal prayer time, and then quietly walk over to the couple and advise them that you would be happy to pray for their request and encourage them to continue in their faithfulness and patience as they wait for God's blessing in having a baby.

9. It is Youth Sunday and all the youth will be serving a luncheon after church service to raise money for their next mission trip. All the youth have taken over the kitchen duties that you and other church members typically execute for such meals. When you walk over to the beverage station, you notice one particular youth member is not keeping up the pace in preparing drinks.

A. You politely go over to the adolescent and present your personal method for preparing drinks, and in doing so, you completely take over without noticing the teen left the beverage station.

B. You take your drink from the teenager, say *"thank you,"* step over the spilled tea on the floor, and find your seat in the dining hall.

C. You notice lots of liquid spilled on the floor, but you are too afraid to say anything to upset the adolescent because his parents are in line behind you.

D. As the teen hands you a drink, you quickly grab it and remark on how long you had to wait in line as well as the amount of melted ice, which caused your soda to taste different.

E. You inform the adolescent, *"Hey, I don't know if anyone told you, but preparing the drinks is the hardest job and you are doing excellent! Keep up the good work. Is there anything I can do to help?"*

PERSONALITY RESULTS

Scoring for this quiz is as easy as A, B, C, and D. So, if you answered with mostly A's, then you most likely exhibit Type A personality traits. If you answered mostly B's, then you are closer to a Type B. If you answered with mostly C's then you are Type C, and if you answered with mostly D's, then you are Type D. If, however you answered with mostly E's, then you are doing pretty well in your Christian walk and are mature in producing fruit, so keep up the excellent work! Did you find out anything interesting about yourself as a Christian after taking this quiz? Or maybe you already know something in your personality needs changing, but you have a difficult time admitting your faults, like me? (Disclosure: I have also found research for individuals having an actual Personality E type, but for this quiz, we will utilize it as the best possible answer.)

Remember, we each respond differently to any given situation. Sometimes we will act like Type B and sometimes Type C, or we may think like Type D but act like Type E—God knows the secrets of our hearts (Psalms 44:21) and knows our thoughts even before we speak them (Psalms 139:4).

One more note about reflecting on your answers: let's say you wanted to grow up to be a school teacher when you were younger, but a random college quiz placed you on another career path based on your answers. You may be totally unhappy and living a life full of regret due to answers given on a simple quiz. Here's the good news—you don't have to feel the same about these quiz results. If you have accepted Jesus Christ as your personal Savior, you are still a precious child of God and will never have your adoption papers revoked—no matter what answers you gave or what personality type you currently are.

You are still a citizen of Heaven!

Thankfully, we have access to our Creator granted by Christ who died for our sins so that we may approach Him and humbly ask for forgiveness when we fail Him or when our actions do not live up to Christian expectations and virtues. We must also be accepting of the Holy Spirit, who many seem to forget lives inside every believer. The Holy Spirit helps us acknowledge biblical Scripture and allows us to embrace God as He molds us into the people we were initially created to be.

Aristotle once said, *"Knowing yourself is the beginning of all wisdom."* This idea is particularly stressed by former authors of many personality theories. I believe, however, that *"fear of the Lord is the beginning of wisdom, and the knowledge of the Holy One is understanding"* (Proverbs 9:10). It is our job to follow the Lord's commands and identify our purpose as Christians to truly understand who He created us to be.

Let's discuss answers to the quiz and subsequent implications as they relate to each of the nine attributes of the fruit of the Spirit.

LOVE

The first quiz question regarding communion is based upon the first mentioned fruit of the Spirit—*Love*. Whenever someone asks a question in relation to the practice of our faith, we should always answer in a kind and loving way and avoid argumentative speech. Questions such as these are opportunities given by God to perhaps plant seeds in the one asking the question. The answer, however, lies in our ability to justify our response, and how do we do that? By reading and meditating in God's Holy Word—the Bible. God spoke to His servant, Joshua, saying:

> *This Book of the Law shall not depart from your mouth, but you shall meditate in it day and night, that you may observe to do according to all that is written in it. For then you will make your way prosperous, and then you will have good success. Have I not commanded you? Be strong and of good courage;*

do not be afraid, nor be dismayed, for the Lord your God is with you wherever you go (Joshua 1:8-9).

The suggestion from this Scripture urges us to study God's Word and not only read it, but actually *speak* its truth. When the verse states *"shall not depart from your mouth,"* God is telling us that in order to be successful, we must *outwardly express* biblical Scripture as we boldly admit to others the many reasons for our faith. Most Christians, including myself and Moses (yes, I just grouped myself with *the* actual Moses), avoid doctrinal discussions with non-believers because we are not always confident in giving the correct answer. Just as Moses had a helper in his brother, Aaron, we also have been given a Helper... the *Holy Spirit*. It is imperative that we not only read the Word, but practice what we are reading. We have the promise from our Heavenly Father that He will be with us no matter the situation or circumstance—all we have to do is study His Word on a regular, daily basis.

If you're like me, we should never look for ulterior motives by the questioner or answer in a demeaning tone, rather seek ways to answer questions with a loving heart when it regards our faith. It is true, some will question us out of evil propaganda, but remember, love is patient and kind and is not easily angered (I Corinthians 13:4-5). And we should *"always be ready to give a defense to everyone who asks [us] a reason for the hope that is in [us],"* which is Christ Jesus (I Peter 3:15). We should always seek ways to talk about our love for Jesus.

For those like myself who have been a Christian for years or maybe even decades and still feel inadequate about sharing your testimony or discussing Scripture, there are various opportunities to promote better understanding of the Word. Examples include teaching a children's Sunday school class, joining a small group, blogging, or perhaps writing a book. I just spoke on spiritual maturity with my Sunday school class, which is full of third-graders—their comprehension is far beyond what mine was at that age. I informed them that because of their faith and knowledge of the Bible, even though they are only eight and nine years old, they are actually more mature than an elderly man or woman who has never believed in Jesus. They were astounded to hear this, and I urged them to continue sharing the love of Jesus with all of their friends at school.

Now, whether you are a child, teenager, young or older adult, always seek ways to talk about your love for Jesus with others, but even better, look for ways to incorporate actual Scripture as the basis of your faith. Those who *"confess that Jesus is the Son of God, God abides in him, and he in God"* (I John 4:15).

JOY

The second quiz question discusses the idea of finding joy in serving. The quiz question was specific to working in the church nursery, but can relate to various roles within the church—roles that may require us to serve above our own desires for the good of the church. What better example than Jesus who did not come to be served, but to serve others (Matthew 20:28)!

However, one might find two types of people within the church—those who give and those who take—OR—those who serve and those who complain.

You know who I am talking about!

Now that my husband is attending seminary school, I am truly seeing the church in a different way. Sure, I teach a children's Sunday school class and sing on the praise team, but now I find myself thinking about our church as a whole. Those who do not make church a priority create difficulty for the congregation to come together as a whole to do God's work. This causes frustration for the leaders of the church and sometimes even undermines their joy in service. Although finding joy in serving at church may be difficult, it may be even more difficult in our everyday lives, but we are assured from Jesus, Himself, that we will see Him again, and no one can take that joy from our hearts (John 16:22).

It's easy to have joy on the weekends or while on vacation, or after a great vacation Bible school or baptism service. And who can deny pure joy at a wedding or the birth of a new baby? When life throws us curveballs, though, we often sink into depression, despair, and even guilt. Sometimes we face tribulation in our lives that takes the focus off of what is really important, such as the Church and those who God has put in our lives to love us. And while Type A's are typically workaholics, we need to concentrate on the actual *quality* of our service for the Lord, and not focus on the *quantity*. For the Bible tells us, *"whatever you do, do it heartily, as to the Lord and not to men"* (Colossians 3:23).

This does *not* translate into *"do as much as you can so others will see."* We are doing the Lord's work for Him, not to impress our peers.

There is a pretty distinct difference between what the world tells us versus what our Heavenly Father tells us. Sure, there are rewards for both, but I would rather focus on the eternal rewards rather than an earthly consolation prize. If we allow guilt, depression, and fleshly desires to lead our hearts and minds, our focus will quickly shift away from all that gives us true joy and peace.

The Book of Romans says, *"Now may the God of hope fill you all with joy and peace in believing, that you may abound in hope by the power of the Holy Spirit"* (15:13). We all lead busy lives, and if you are a Type A individual, then you are the operator behind your busy schedule. However, we should be bold in our service for the Lord and prioritize our time focusing on the Church, which bring us joy and peace within our souls—a true joy this world will never fulfill and that earthly circumstances will never change.

PEACE

This brings us to the third quiz question, which relates to keeping the peace among the church. The question discusses financial concerns regarding a youth conference and the various answers depict either agreement or frustration between the congregation and the leaders of the church. The Book of Timothy states, *"For the love of money is a root of all kinds of evil, for which some have strayed from the faith in their greediness, and pierced themselves through with many sorrows"* (I Timothy 6:10).

This question does not focus on the various functions supported by the church, but rather the ensured peace and harmony within the church and with its leaders. We are instructed to *"Obey those who rule over you, and be submissive, for they watch out for your souls, as those who must give account. Let them do so with joy and not with grief, for that would be unprofitable for you"* (Hebrews 13:17). The implications in this verse are very powerful.

We are to be submissive, or compliant, with our leaders' decisions. We should *never* approach the leaders of our church with aggression and hostility just because we may disagree with their decisions. On the other hand, leaders must also exhibit peace as they endure unnecessary opposition from those who may not always agree with them. For they also submit to an authority figure, who is God the Father, and they are required to give an account for all of their decisions based upon His name.

Yes, it is true that the leaders of our churches are human, but they have not accepted a position of leadership lightly. They may not always do the right things as we see fit, but the elders and leaders guide their decisions for the church after much prayer and devotion. And, as fellow members of various congregations, we should pray for them and for God to bless them with the right answers as they seek the Lord's will—this includes all who are in leadership positions within our governments as well. Sure, they may ask for opinions or take a vote on trivial things such as scheduling of events or ideas for missions; however, we should never cause dissension within the church just because of a disagreement, unless their ruling is against biblical Scripture.

The Book of Hebrews counsels us not to cause grief or add distress to our leaders, as this would not be to our benefit and could be detrimental in our Christian walk. Instead, Jesus' brother tells us *"Now the fruit of righteousness is sown in peace by those who make peace"* (James 3:18). We are advised to *"keep the unity of the Spirit in the bond of peace"* as we are one in the body and one in the Spirit of Christ (Ephesians 4:3-4). In order to prevent dissension within the church, we must eliminate our pride and unite as one in *peace.*

PATIENCE

Patience is the means by which we can improve all of the attributes of the fruit discussed so far as well as those yet to be mentioned. The fourth quiz question relates not so much to leaders, but learning to embrace actual leadership within the church. I'm sure we can recall a time when maybe our family, friends, or co-workers were not in-tune with our own desires. However, patience is a key virtue for any believer to develop within the church, specifically for its leaders. Question four specifically poses various behaviors which were met by the leadership team with an unexpected decision. While we all esteem to have the best behavior, sometimes life throws us for a loop, and our conduct does not always display our fruit to the best of our ability, especially in the heat of the moment. This is where the term *"practice makes perfect"* comes into play.

And how do we develop patience? Well, with more practice.

Years ago, I remember coming home after work and complaining to my husband about my work environment. He quickly quoted me a Bible verse, which is now probably my favorite verse as it applies to both my life as a health care professional and my service within the church. It states *"Let us not grow weary while doing good, for in due season we shall reap if we do not lose heart. Therefore, as we have opportunity, let us do good to all, especially to those who are of the household of faith"* (Galatians 6:10). Rare is the Type A individual who actually likes the unexpected, unless it is an unexpected vacation to Hawaii. We dislike changes within our work, school, home, and even our church. Fortunately, change is required to grow. Unfortunately, we are often not content with what we have. *Remember, bigger is not always better.*

Believers within the church must show respect for the leaders of the church and be appreciative of their efforts and the decisions made on their behalf (Hebrews 13:17). Serving as a leader is very demanding because one not only strives to fulfill certain obligations, but must also lead by example, especially for potential leaders who may serve in the future (Hebrews 13:18). While those with Type A may not have enjoyed playing *"Follow the Leader"* as a child, we *do* need to follow our leaders within our churches. In fact, the Book of Hebrews teaches us this very principle. We are not only to show respect, but also to pray for the leaders of our church (Hebrews 13:18).

If our sole purpose in attending a church is based upon decisions of trivial matters, then we need to decide *why* we are attending church in the first place? No church building is perfect. They have the same cracks and holes as any other building in our communities. However, the purpose it maintains in gathering as a place of worship is the ultimate reason for its existence. If we can acknowledge that the church itself is built on the resurrected Son of God, Jesus Christ, only then can we develop patience and a passion to maintain and grow the church's mission for evangelism.

God created patience as a virtue because He was and still is the model for absolute patience. He continues to love us despite our habitual failures. In turn, we should extend that same patience to others and continue to show appreciation for their service in growing the Church.

KINDNESS

The fifth question brings us to an interesting fruit—*kindness*, specifically in regards to caring for those within the church. This question in the quiz relates to the church members' compassion toward their injured pastor. The Gospel of Luke states that kindness is a behavior or manner in which we treat others without expecting anything in return (6:35). Kindness is becoming a recent phenomenon with various new movie and book releases. The movie, *Wonder*, teaches children the importance of showing kindness by looking on the inside rather than bullying those with different appearances. A quote from the book states, *"We carry with us, as human beings, not just the capacity to be kind, but the very choice of kindness."*[43] Thus, kindness is a fruit that all cultures can choose to display, not just those who believe in Jesus Christ. If the entire world considered true kindness, surely peace would abound. Our lives may significantly improve on earth, but eternal salvation would still be in question for those who have not accepted Christ as their Savior. So, how can one tell the difference between a Christian and a non-Christian who show kindness to others? The difference is that our fruit is rooted in Christ our Savior.

We all know the golden rule, which comes from the Gospel of Matthew and states do unto others as you would have them do to you (7:12). Each of us has the ability to show respect and appreciation toward others—even non-believers have honorable morals and may show more kindness than some Christians. Unfortunately, they are not promised the same rewards as we who carry our faith in Jesus Christ. We choose to show loving kindness to others because He first loved us (I John 4:19). Sure, we must be willing to show true kindness to those within the church, but we also are challenged to serve those on the outside, especially when our fruit may not be appreciated or recognized. God doesn't place priority on showing kindness to anyone who holds a leadership position, such as the preacher mentioned in the quiz question. He does expect us to focus on all of His children—even those who do not acknowledge Him as Father.

Christians sometimes prioritize certain acts of kindness to those closest to them, but often forget serving outside of their comfort zone. The first Book of Timothy teaches these principles on how to treat those within the church, specifically widows and elders (Ch. 5), but also the orphans and the poor.

We are to be *"an example to the believers in word, in conduct, in love, in spirit, in faith, [and] in purity"* (I Timothy 4:12). Jesus also taught that we should treat those outside our biological families just the same.[44] As Christians, we are members of the family of God, which ultimately directs our priorities into sharing fruit with all of God's children—both believers and non-believers.

So, how can we tell the difference between Christians versus non-Christians in regards to kindness? Jesus tells us the answer in the Gospel of Luke when He mentions to His believers that sinners love those who love them, they do good to those who are good to them, and they lend to those who will return back; but we as Christians are to *"love [our] enemies, do good, and lend, hoping for nothing in return. Our reward will be great, and [we] will be the sons of the Most High; for [even] He is kind to the unthankful and evil. Therefore, be merciful, just as your Father is merciful"* (Luke 6:32-36). Now, it's important to note that the term *"sinners"* is not just a title for non-believers. We *all* sin and come short of the glory of God; this verse is inclusive for each of us, even Christians (Romans 3:23).

It is very difficult for Type A Christians to perform tasks without receiving any recognition, and this includes random acts of kindness. Sometimes, our personality traits compel us into demonstrating our fruit only to receive admiration from those who see our unexpected acts of service. However, in reality we have been planning (or possibly scheming) how to put our fruit on display for others to appreciate. We may even anticipate congratulatory responses for our kindness, which only fuels our fire in continuing our services; this is much worse than others, even non-believers, who choose to show random acts of kindness. God teaches us throughout the Bible that even though our fruit may go unnoticed and even be rejected, He will graciously welcome us into Heaven for an eternity along with many rewards for our services here on earth. This may be the most difficult task in improving ourselves as Type A Christians, in not only learning to avoid premeditated acts of services but to also love those who may not appreciate our fruit. As mentioned in the previous quote, we all have the spirit of kindness within us; we just have to be open to sharing it with others we meet along the way.

As we spontaneously show kindness to those we love, we must also show mercy to our rivals, even if they are in our families or church congregations. Once we understand that our family is not marked by blood, color, or culture, but instead includes all who are created by God, then we can show the world the compassion that was first shown to us by Jesus—and that is the mark of true Christian loving kindness.

GOODNESS

Our sixth question discusses the idea of goodness in regards to the clean-up day at church in which one's behavior could range from task-oriented to self-isolation. Type A individuals most often view the worst in others and prefer feelings of personal achievement to having a relationship with others.[45] Finding goodness in someone is a rare jewel in today's society. We live in a dog-eat-dog world where many people try to climb their way to the top no matter who they hurt in the process.

So why do we feel the need to step over others at church, and why is it sometimes so hard to appreciate others for their service?

The answer is simple: As Type A's, we think we can do it better, so we don't ask anyone for help. And sometimes we see serving in the church as a job or a chore rather than as actual *service* the way God intended. We must first learn to acknowledge others for who they are and why it is important to work together as one body. Next, we must focus on the needs and goals of righteous services or acts for the church. If the body of Christ cannot work together on a simple service project with fellow believers, then how will we work together on a much larger scale—like planning a mission trip or organizing a relief effort.

Most of us like being able to provide a service for the church; however, we often like to work alone or not allow someone else to serve us. It is equally important not to disregard a fellow brother or sister who is trying to utilize their fruit, even if we are the recipients of such love offerings.

One of our local Christian radio stations, WCQR, promotes the idea of paying it forward in their *"Drive-Thru Difference,"* which allows you to pay for the person behind you at various restaurants on the first Monday of each month.[46] Unfortunately, some on social media admit to being offended by this gesture. These individuals felt insulted that a complete stranger in front of them *believed* they were unable to pay for their meal (even though that is not the intent); and they also felt pressure to pay for the person behind them.

Why is it so difficult to be a grateful recipient of such blessings? The simple, five-letter word, P-R-I-D-E, *Pride,* is our own worst enemy in accepting the good fruit of others. We all have different talents, but when it comes time for us to receive a blessing, sometimes we choose to be ungrateful, which coincidentally can drive a Type A person senseless if we feel that our good works are not appreciated.

Therefore, it is imperative that we both accept and utilize the fruit of the Spirit to guide us on our Christian walk rather than leaning on our own personalities and behaviors based on our own preferences or circumstances. We are all going to face times of stress and turmoil because we live in a world full of evil, but we cannot lose faith in the One who is our Shepherd to pull us through. Just as David spoke in the Book of Psalms, *"Yea, though I walk through the valley of the shadow of death, I will fear no evil; For you are with me...surely goodness and mercy shall follow me all the days of my life"* (23:4-6). While we need to ensure we set examples of goodness for others within the church and non-believers, we also need to *accept, acknowledge,* and *appreciate* the kind acts of others bestowed upon us as part of the blessings that come with being one in the body of Christ.

MEEKNESS

The next question within the personality quiz deals with Christians with a past—oh wait, that's all of us! The question discussed the meek testimony of a Christian woman who sacrificed her pride and humbled herself unto the congregation but was met with contentious and hypocritical judgment. Even those of us saved at an early age are still committing sins despite our Christian conversions. It is essential to maintain appreciation for all of our brothers and sisters in Christ no matter the circumstance in which they humbly fell under God's amazing grace.

When Dr. David Jeremiah spoke on meekness as it was expressed by our Savior, he described meekness as an action directed toward those who are helpless and never directed at oneself.[47] He spoke of various situations as Jesus displayed the vast differences between humility and righteous behavior. In the temple, Jesus became very angry in His actions toward the unrighteous Pharisees and Sadducees who took advantage of fellow Jews and Gentiles who came to worship. Jesus later provided an example of complete humility as He faced the Sanhedrin and *"kept silent"* when questioned in the courts (Matthew 26:63).

Meekness was further displayed as Jesus was condemned to death and hung on the cross, not for *His* sins, but for mine and yours. He was obedient to His Heavenly Father, remaining humble as He put each and every one of us before Himself, all the while asking forgiveness of His accusers (Luke 23:34).

All of our sins, both small and large, were covered by the blood of Jesus. By His grace and mercy, we have been forgiven and been made righteous through His sacrifice. Jesus provides a great example of humility and demonstrates the type of love we should have for others, especially those who do not have a voice or who are weak in the spirit. As Type A Christians, it is very difficult to show dependence on anyone because (1) we feel that we can do everything better ourselves, and (2) we feel that asking for help shows weakness. It is important to learn that humility is not a sign of weakness but a true sign of reliance on our Lord and Savior.

While God already knows our thoughts, He still wants us to come to Him with our needs and concerns. We should be quick to admit to ourselves, as well as to others, that we need God in our lives. Once we realize the importance of humility in our own relationship with God, then we can understand fellow Christians who show true humility instead of viewing them as weak. As believers, we are challenged to suffer with other Christians when they face trials and rejoice when they are exalted (I Corinthians 12:26). We have been taught to pray for one another, embrace one another, forgive one another, grieve with one another, and most importantly, love one another. When one person hurts, the entire church should ache, and when one soul is saved, the entire church should rejoice.

Paul writes in the Book of Galatians, we are to bear one another's burdens, which are sins committed inadvertently (6:1-2). We as Christians should continue to edify one another just as Jesus demonstrated on the cross when He saved the sinner facing the same cruel death. We are to show mercy and grace to *all*—no matter the sin and no matter the age of the sinner.

It seems we are often quick to forgive those who are younger in their offenses, but what about mature Christians who allows themselves to travel down the road of sin? What forgiveness do we afford them? Are we all not sinners? How will others see each of us as we stumble and fall? Jesus did not humble Himself for only those troubled in their youth. He humbly died for all of us, even those considered mature in the faith. When someone gives their testimony, whether at church or work or even at a ballgame, we need to offer the utmost respect and honor to those who pour out their hearts and souls as they proudly exclaim how Almighty God saved them from a life of trouble, just as He did for us all.

Don't be afraid to share what obstacle God helped you overcome in your life and the love you felt when other Christians embraced you into their family of believers. When we hear someone criticizing another believer's testimony, my prayer is that we each witness to them by quoting a few of the scriptures mentioned in this book. Consider a time when you did not feel embraced by the body of Christ? Did you feel loved and accepted as a sinner, or did you feel rejected from those who thought they were better than you? When we judge others, we may exclude them from a family (something they may never have had before) and possibly push them away from having a relationship with God. It is essential that we encourage others to offer their testimony even when they are far from perfect, because none of us are perfect.

If we are going to be proud about anything, let's be proud of God's grace, mercy, and love. And, finally, just as Dr. Jeremiah taught, let's ensure that our quality of meekness is utilized not just to protect ourselves, but to defend others who cannot defend themselves—we may at times be the only one in a room representing Jesus. Will we be ready to come to His defense? After all, He defended each of us on the cross.

FAITHFULNESS

The next to last question on the quiz affects each of us in regards to not only maintaining our faith but encouraging other believers when they are facing tribulation. We can all attest to having faith when times are going well, but when the storms hit, our faithfulness may become weak and require persistent encouragement. This quiz question relates to a young married couple who requests prayer from their family of believers with hopes of becoming pregnant.

Although my husband and I endured years of infertility, I was constantly searching for physiologic and scientific reasons for our inability to conceive. Unfortunately, no physician, including myself, could determine any possible causes. I admit that my faith wavered as I felt like God was not hearing my prayers—mostly because He wasn't answering in the way or time that *I* desired.

I remember one Sunday during church when I cried out in front of my church congregation asking for prayers as I so badly wanted to have a second child. While I know my church members prayed for me and my husband, we never conceived a second or third child, which means our daughter will never know what it's like to grow up with a sibling. I know that sometimes our prayers are answered in ways we never expect, but it is very difficult when you first learn the answer is, *"No."*

I am reminded of a verse in the Book of Psalms, which tells us that *"It is better to trust in the Lord than to put confidence in man"* (118:8). While I believe that God has blessed many physicians with the ability to heal and treat individuals with various illnesses and disabilities, these providers are *never* meant to take the place of our faith in our Heavenly Father. I realize now that I should have placed *all* of my faith in the ultimate Healer and trusted His timeline. Now that I am currently working as a provider in obstetrics, I am able to better sympathize with patients afflicted with the same problems that I faced. I pray that I am able to offer them hope and encouragement when medical treatments fail.

Sometimes, God actually reveals to us why our prayers were *not* answered. For example, have you ever wondered why a certain relationship ended *until* you met your perfect soul mate and then your previous feelings of sadness and disappointment were overcome through love and hope? Or have you ever felt cheated out of a job only to find out there was a superior position in a dream location waiting just for you? These are the moments when God encourages us to be patient and to understand He is hard at work. He wants nothing but the best for all of His children, no matter their age.

On the other hand, we may never discover why our prayers went unanswered. It is difficult to remain faithful in God when our prayers are not answered the way we anticipated, but that is exactly what God wants us to do. He wants us to put our faith in Him and trust His perfect will for our lives. Just as Jesus spoke to His disciples, *"With men this is impossible, but with God all things are possible"* (Matthew 19:26).

Fortunately, researching biblical Scripture for this book has helped me realize the importance of keeping my focus on God. He is the guide for my Christian walk, and I am not to focus on others or compare their blessings with my own. In not having my prayer answered with the conception of another child, I could portray a negative testimony for others to see, but I have chosen to live out a testimony pleasing to God rather than to myself finding the good in all of my life experiences. For example, my daughter now reaps the benefits of having more one-on-one time with me and her dad, at least until she becomes a teenager and wants nothing to do with us!

Often when things do not go our way, we can feel more than just sad—it can be emotionally exhausting. *"But without faith it is impossible to please [God], for He who comes to God must believe that He is, and that He is a rewarder of those who diligently seek Him"* (Hebrews 11:6). Sometimes we will encounter both believers and non-believers who often lack faith during strenuous seasons of life. We may not always be able to sympathize with the events occurring in their lives, but we can choose to share our testimonies of faith and how God can work on their behalf as well.

The goal of question eight was to draw attention to restoring our personal faith in God and edifying others with specific requests. We may not always understand the prayers or desires of those within our family of believers, but as fellow Christians, we are taught *"to comfort... and edify one another"*

(I Thessalonians 5:11) and *"that we may be able to comfort those who are in any trouble, with the comfort with which we ourselves are comforted by God"* (2 Corinthians 1:4). Instead of focusing on blatant judgment and selfish criticism of others, we should first exalt them in prayer and then seek ways to encourage continued faithfulness. And no matter the circumstances or end results, we should always seek ways to glorify our Heavenly Father through the righteousness of faith and bearing of fruit.

SELF-CONTROL

The final quiz question focuses on maintaining self-control. Have you ever wondered why self-control is the last-mentioned fruit of the Spirit? Well, if you are like me, I have always thought of the other attributes as actions we direct toward others, whereas self-control is a fruit based on our internal actions despite a specific cause or event. Sure, it's easy to show love when we're surrounded by family and friends, joy is easily expressed in times of happiness, peace can be conveyed without saying a word, goodness is merely following the principles taught in the Bible, kindness is expressed when performing a service without expecting anything in return, and meekness is displayed when life throws us a curve as we learn to rely more on God. Nonetheless, self-control can be visualized as an actual personality trait, especially if viewed by others as negative.

I believe self-control is mentioned last as it is necessary to utilize all of the previously mentioned fruit of the Spirit—love, joy, peace, patience, kindness, goodness, meekness, and faithfulness. It is vital in maintaining the practice of these eight attributes to improve our self-control. While living in the flesh, this virtue of restraint was best demonstrated by our Savior Jesus Christ in various situations, particularly when He was being judged and condemned by His own people. Those who possess Type A personalities become their own worst enemies when it comes to self-control.

We are typically very organized and profess self-discipline as our lives are planned out to the smallest detail; however, when a little piece of our desired timeline fails, our lives crumble before us and all of our traits are affected. We become easily angered, impatient, impulsive, and even distant to those we love the most as we try to restore what has been destroyed. We forget as Type A Christians that we have a Supreme Power living within us that helps us along life's unexpected turns. We forget to live by God's timeline instead of our own. We forget to pray for guidance from our Helper. We forget to apply the Scripture to our lives during tumultuous times. And we forget our fruit is affected merely because we have lost control of our lives. Fortunately, we have Jesus as a role model to demonstrate the righteous act of self-control, and we can read about many biblical characters who also suffered a lack of self-control and how God continued to use them to fulfill His purpose. Most of us who try to maintain self-control are desperately trying to fulfill our goals, but God will always direct our paths and set our priorities in order, if we let Him.

A few synonyms for the term *"self-control"* include restraint, discipline, and willpower. Unfortunately, these are all terms I am not particularly fond of, especially when it comes to exercise. On the other hand, my husband is probably the most disciplined person that I have ever met, aside from my father-in-law who passed down this formidable trait. They both show discipline in various ways, including exercise, nutrition (for the most part), and work-related organization. However, I can assure you my husband is not disciplined in *every* aspect of his life. He is not a lazy person by any means, but his priorities are what drives his intentions.

Years ago in high school, athletics took priority over his studies, but now his focus has shifted as his seminary education is currently taking precedence. His ability to hold his tongue (self-restraint) is much better than mine. I unfortunately suffer from the disease of saying foolish things before truly thinking of their implications. I have at times been utterly embarrassed for not learning to restrain myself in conversations with others, and I have learned as a provider to talk less and listen more—something I am trying to do with family and friends, although I'm not sure how well I am doing.

Although self-control is somewhat easy to maintain in front of strangers, we don't always practice this fruit with those we love the most. Sometimes we say rude and hurtful things, including remarks about someone's weight, age, color of hair, lack of intelligence or education, and even judgmental comments concerning the activities of family members or close friends. Self-restraint and self-control are knowledgeable virtues that require practice just like the other eight attributes. We should always keep the thoughts of others in mind when speaking to not only avoid confrontation on a personal level but to also avoid conflict on a much grander scale, such as an entire church.

Regardless of spiritual maturity, Christians are viewed as role models by the younger generations who are yearning to be molded. If we cannot maintain self-control over our own lives and relationships with others, then we are not very good teachers. This specific quiz question is related to those who feel threatened within their roles of the church. We should always appreciate, encourage, and show honor to those who will be our future leaders. We are taught not to be wise in our own opinions (Romans 12:16) because change is inevitable. Change is not always a bad thing when it comes to serving God. We can never outserve God, and we should never criticize others who try to serve God in ways unlike our own.

There are various questions I could have chosen regarding self-control, including marriage, parenting, finances, witnessing, etc. But with any topic, it is imperative to discipline ourselves for the purpose of godliness. *"For bodily exercise profits a little, but godliness is profitable for all things, having promise of the life that now is and of that which is to come"* (I Timothy 4:8). With a strong foundation of biblical Scripture and a fervent prayer life, when we face the unexpected, we are to remember that *"God has not given us a spirit of fear, but of power and of love and of a sound mind"* (2 Timothy 1:7). We must value the fruit of self-control as this virtue will set us apart from non-believers, especially when placed in difficult situations.

While we are not perfect, we will utterly fail at one time or another and should always strive to be more like Christ who perfected this quality through His selfless actions on this earth.

WHY DOES THIS QUIZ MATTER?

The true reason for taking this personality quiz was to see how you typically interact with other Christians, and to identify necessary improvements before witnessing to non-believers. The fruit of the Spirit is fully attainable by each and every Christian believer in whom Jesus Christ lives. Jesus told his disciples:

> *I am the vine, you are the branches. He who abides in Me, and I in him, bears much fruit; for without Me you can do nothing... If you abide in Me, and My words abide in you, you will ask what you desire, and it shall be done for you. By this My Father is Glorified, that you bear much fruit; so you will be My disciples (John 15: 5, 7).*

There are various personalities present within every church. Never look down upon those who are not as outgoing in the church (Type B's). While some of us may be louder than others (Type A's), we can *all* serve the Lord in a multitude of ways. We should continually pray for all members to have the courage to speak and be confident in their faith (Type C's). And always remember the need for mature Christians to exhibit spiritual fruit for others to observe and model (Type D's). Through writing this book, I have learned that I have jealous tendencies toward those who may have attained a fruit I have yet to achieve, which as a Christian may be detrimental to my walk if I'm always comparing myself to others, positively or negatively.

The question becomes how do we continue to glorify God while restoring our fruit?

We must first seek a relationship with Him through reading the Bible, consistently praying, and continued praise and worship. We are to honor God in all we do and say. If we have faith in His Son and have accepted Christ as our Savior, then God will continue to prune us so that we may produce more fruit (John 15:2). However, for those who do not read the Word routinely, nor appreciate the specific gifts they have available, they will never reach their full potentials.

In an attempt to learn more about ourselves, we often come to realize our shortcomings. Do you remember Saul, the hostile Jewish Pharisee, who sought to kill Jewish-Christians? He discovered his true identity on his way to Damascus where he was converted to Christianity by none other than Jesus who questioned Saul's true character. Upon accepting his new role as evangelist, Saul, whose name was later mentioned as Paul, continued to fulfill his calling until death. He, above all the apostles, realized the struggle between the flesh and the spirit. Paul spoke, *"For what I am doing, I do not understand. For what I will to do, that I do not practice; but what I hate, that I do"* (Romans 7:15).

Have you ever really sat back and thought about what Paul's statement means for you? A church letter board sign recently declared, *"Practice makes perfect, be careful what you practice!"* And that is the epitome of what Paul was trying to say.

We must ensure that the skills we are trying to perfect are right in the sight of God who never fails to offer grace regardless of our shortcomings.

His statement is very important as it relates to the same goal we strive to meet every day as Christians. We hope our actions match our fruitful spirits, but unfortunately, even as Christians, our flesh sometimes takes over. Family, friends, and even co-workers observe our behaviors and responses when adversity comes our way. Thankfully, through Christ Jesus, we are *"made free from the law of sin and death"* and God's grace is poured out on us as His followers (Romans 8:1).

Can you imagine the Gentile nations observing the disciples arguing during the early formation of the church? What if their beliefs were compromised because the disciples did not practice what they preached? Do you think the Gentiles would have believed their testimony if they were impatient, angry, or exhibited behaviors contrary to their message of love? Would Jews or Gentiles have trusted followers of Jesus if they had *not* left everything behind to follow Him... even to their deaths?

What a testimony to Jesus' followers!

That is similar to our current situation in today's society. We often try to push our practice of *religion* on others who may actually be better doers of the Word than we are. So then why shouldn't we learn how to become better witnesses for Christ? It is my strong belief that many Christians argue over items that are irrelevant, which causes dissension amongst church members. This is considered a great achievement in the eyes of our enemy. The devil would like nothing better than to have

God's adopted children fight over trivial issues which takes our focus away from our mission of witnessing to non-believers. Discussions quickly lead to arguments in the church setting, such as decisions regarding chairs versus pews, traditional music over contemporary, or one particular Bible version over another. Instead, we should focus on evangelical issues, such as singing to those who are unable to attend worship service, delivering Bibles to those in need, and perhaps taking the time to read with them.

How are we ever going to fulfill the Great Commission to spread the love of Christ if we cannot agree on methods for accomplishing our mission? We must understand that actions speak far louder than words, as evidenced by the disciples who laid down their lives for Christ.

Hopefully this quiz can teach us how to edify others of the faith and then offer our fruitful service to non-believers in the same. Christians embody various personality traits, and while God may lead our lives in various directions, there are benefits to having certain personality traits—even those who are Type A! In the following chapter, we will learn how to use our Type A strengths at school and work, in the home as a spouse and parent, and especially in our Christian walk. Learning to overcome the negative traits as mentioned in the quiz is essential to living a life for God. Now, let's see if we can utilize our Type A traits in fulfilling God's purpose as Christians.

CHAPTER THREE
TYPE A PERSONALITY BENEFITS

Despite all the negative traits previously mentioned, there are *many* benefits to having a Type A personality. God created each of us with different backgrounds, cultures, talents, and even personalities, which all combine to makes us unique. We should be thankful to God for allowing us to be different and not one and the same. Furthermore, we should always seek to improve ourselves and understand the purpose for our specific traits. God created us for His glory, and by trying to act like someone we are not, we are only failing His will and plans for our lives.

While none of us are created exactly the same, individuals with Type A do share similar personality tendencies, which lead others to group us as a whole. Therefore, in order to use our Type A personalities to the best of our abilities, we must reach our full potential by learning how to enhance our fruit. Only then will we see the benefits for being a Type A Christian.

In this chapter, we will learn the necessary measures needed to enhance our personalities as we seek guidance from the Holy Spirit. Next, we will discuss advantages and benefits of having a Type A personality in our everyday lives as students, employees, and spouses. And last, we will discover how to utilize our personalities to the fullest in our Christian walk—even using some of our most negative traits to our spiritual advantage that will bless our own lives and the lives of others.

Unfortunately, we live in a world full of critics. Others tell us who to be, how to act, what to like, and how to live. The Book of Romans tells us, *"do not be conformed to this world, but be transformed by the renewing of your mind, that you may prove what is that good and acceptable and perfect will of God"* (12:2). David Jeremiah further clarifies this verse in that *"to be **transformed** is to go from the **inside out** and to be **conformed** is to go from the **outside in**."* This suggests that as sinners saved by grace, we have the Holy Spirit to control our fleshly desires, actions, and personalities. Our behavior must change from the inside out by the help of the Holy Spirit as we further our knowledge of our Heavenly Father through consistent prayer and reading of His Word.

Only God can change our bad personality traits molded by mankind into good traits renewed by the Holy Spirit. Just as it is written in Isaiah, *"we are the clay, and You our Potter, and all we are the work of Your hand"* (64:8). Once we realize God's will for our lives and understand our purpose in sharing the Gospel, only then will we be able to resist being conformed by worldly pleasures. Therefore, Christians should learn to identify and embrace who God created us to be, but also improve upon our learned, secular personality traits that counteract the personalities God meant for us to develop.

Dr. Charles Stanley with In Touch Ministries was speaking on the radio regarding personalities of Christians. In paraphrasing, he jokingly mentioned that our personalities will follow us to Heaven, and hopefully our personalities will be likeable for others to enjoy for *all* of eternity. Can you imagine living with various Christians in Heaven that you may dread seeing at church because they have a poor attitude? If we are to spend an eternity together, then we should at least try to get along with one another, especially those who worship within the same church sanctuary. We are told in the first Book of Corinthians that *"there are diversities of gifts, but [we are to have] the same Spirit"* (12:4). This means that we all have special talents; hence, we should seek ways to identify the good in others rather than their weaknesses as we work together for God's purpose.

The Holy Spirit who lives in *all* believers allows us to show the same love and forgiveness that Jesus demonstrated while on earth. Therefore, our personality plays a huge role in how we witness to others, and it is important to realize how our negative behavior can impact both believers and non-believers.

We share the Gospel of Jesus Christ and the grace of God with others by how we act, how we respond, and how we treat others in order to further the Kingdom of God. It is also equally important to develop our personalities into something that God and our brothers and sisters in Christ can enjoy for eternity. I don't know of anyone who enjoys being around others who display negative or sarcastic personalities. While we face many trials and tribulations while on this earth, believers should consistently display attitudes of true joy with the hope of glory in spending eternity with our Creator.

Once we allow the Holy Spirit to transform our personalities, only then can we produce fruitful, beneficial traits. As born-again Christians, it is imperative to read the Bible and learn to imitate those who were true followers of Christ in order to set examples for today's society. Until we realize the importance of our relationships with fellow believers and in leading others to Christ, we may never understand the benefits for having such strong personality features.

When I was a new mother and just returning to work from maternity leave, I found myself in utter despair. At the time, I was also working on my graduate degree, trying to maintain a full schedule with work, school, cooking, cleaning, and breastfeeding. I felt like I was losing control of our house and I started to feel overwhelmed. One day, I was searching online and found *FlyLady.net*. The website offers advice on how to clean, organize, and declutter a house.[48] I immediately fell in love with the website as the female creator must definitely be a Type A individual.

I was amazed by its organization and use of descriptive charts, monthly habits, and even cleaning zones for keeping a tidy house. The recommendations involved a *"Baby Step"* process to establish good habits and prevent a sense of overwhelming guilt in completing everyday chores, which otherwise could lead to an entire weekend of cleaning.[49] Well, just like a fad diet, I really tried to adhere to the website's recommendations, but I eventually failed, most likely during my husband's baseball season when I am seldom at home. This is, however, a Type A's dream website, and I highly recommend it if you are looking for advice on cleanliness and organization skills for the home.

I did, however, learn a valuable lesson from this website: Prior to truly deep cleaning a house, the owner must first *declutter.*

Interesting thought—before you can truly clean or purify, you must first *declutter* or provide *"space."*

I realized that just as we must declutter our house to truly clean it, so it is in our Christian walk. We must first declutter our lives to fully allow God to deep clean our souls. We must hand Him all of our sins, our doubts, our failures, our fears, and our regrets. Only then can we allow the Holy Spirit to take over our flesh and purify us from within. Our personalities can be like chameleons as we take on new identities based upon given situations, but we have to remain righteous, especially in times of despair and tribulation. It is only when we fully trust and obey God that our souls will be fully decluttered and our fruit can mature.

One author suggests, *"Type A personality characteristics are more of a reaction to environmental factors, or tendencies toward certain behaviors, and are influenced by culture and job structure."*[50] The author later discusses methods for treating or improving characteristics by altering one's *"thinking patterns to more positive ones,"* and by making *"conscious choice[s]"* in changing our lifestyles and behaviors.[51]

Well, that's interesting. We have already discussed how to alter or transform one's thinking pattern, and that is by asking the Holy Spirit to guide our thoughts, actions, behaviors, and perhaps even ask to change the environmental factors around us. One way we can ensure beneficial conscious choices and positive thinking is by starting each day with prayer and Scripture readings. Do you believe our *"thinking patterns"* would be more positive after reading our Bibles *or* after scrolling through negative social media? Learning to declutter our minds will be difficult, but it is essential if we want to grow in the Word and restore our fruit. Consider getting fired from your job. This could be devastating to any family, but if the greater good is to improve your situation in time, then you must count it as a blessing from God who loves you so much that He wants you to be surrounded by those who positively influence you in your everyday life (Romans 8:28).

In claiming my Type A personality, I clearly inherited many traits from my parents who modeled certain behaviors in their everyday lives. They both worked long hours on the job, but always took time to enjoy vacations from their hard work. My parents were quick to provide for those who were in need, such as raising money for St. Jude Children's Hospital, taking homemade chow-chow to a loved one (in the south, chow-chow is eaten with soup beans), or being a source of knowledge to others—my dad was a general contractor and my mom works at one of the largest credit unions in the state of Tennessee. They frequently offer advice for free based upon their expertise.

My brother and I were witnesses to many of their behaviors—the good and the bad—but we both learned the value of a dollar, as well as the benefits of and blessings in serving others. While most with Type A personalities do not tend to enjoy their successes, my parents always ensured that my brother and I reaped their blessings through many vacations. We knew that God provided our fun times together (now and then) because of my parents' obedience to the Lord. We also understood the importance of tithing, which is giving back only a small portion of what God has first given to us.

Now that we know how to transform and declutter through the help of the Holy Spirit, let's discuss the actual benefits of having a Type A personality as a child, employee, family member, and most importantly as a follower of Christ.

BENEFITS OF A TYPE A CHILD, STUDENT, AND ATHLETE

Many individuals benefit from having a Type A personality, including those who are great competitors. They excel in school, sports, home, and work. They enjoy being social and join as many clubs as possible to learn as many skills as they can. They are usually the leaders on the playground, directing their friends in games and helping everyone on their team to succeed so they can win. Young Type A's also enjoy teaching others and performing skills they have already mastered to perfection. And while they may become angry when others do not want to play with them, it is merely because they are so interested in a specific task or game that they can't imagine why others do not feel the same.

Students with Type A personalities do not typically procrastinate. They work on projects as soon as the teacher sends home the instruction sheet and ensure that their parents have everything on the list so they can work on the next project. They take pride in having perfect attendance and report cards. They tend to stay focused on all tasks until their projects are completed, and you will probably have a hard time putting them to bed until they feel they are at a good stopping point.[52] These Type A's also love to talk and tell others about their day and about the goals they have met.

Similarly, Type A athletes almost never quit mid-season. They stick with a sport until they complete their goals, which are attributed to time and practice spent on perfecting the skills needed. They work diligently until the very last game to obtain the prize. They love to seek attention, especially after scoring a basketball goal or stealing the ball from another player.[53] And, from my personal experience, children and athletes with Type A behaviors typically grow and maintain Type A tendencies for the rest of their lives.

Many of these characteristics prove to be valuable as these children eventually serve as leaders in their future careers due to the success they have experienced in the past. And, if children are raised in God-centered homes, then they will have opportunities to be great leaders for Christ in the future. Think of your strong-willed child and how difficult it is to alter his or her beliefs. For children who are saved at earlier ages, they may be able to reach others, both young and old, through their boldness in faith. This may include family members or friends who previously disregarded Christian witnesses, even those closest to them.

My husband and I have similar stories about the affects we both had on the health of our grandparents. When I was between four and six years of age, I persuaded my maternal grandmother to stop smoking with a shiny quarter. And, guess what, she stopped! Around the same time on a Maggie Valley chairlift, my husband who about the same age asked the same of his paternal grandfather, and guess what? He stopped smoking as well! While both have passed to their eternal homes in Heaven, I know that from our specific actions, we were able to further their lives here on earth with just our humble requests. This not only impacted our grandparents, but also other family and friends who were able to cherish them for years to come, including many great-grandchildren.

Now consider if your child was to have the same effect on non-believers but with an even better offer for eternal life. Never, ever discredit anyone's potential for influence as an adopted child of God! God uses us at any age to fulfill his purpose. Consider it a blessing for your child to be spiritually mature with a desire to learn more about God. We must realize, however, that *their* maturity comes at a cost for their parents. Likewise, parents are to be bold in the faith and diligent in studying God's Word in order to encourage and edify our children whom God has called.

BENEFITS OF A TYPE A EMPLOYEE

As Type A children discover success, they learn to crave it in other areas of their lives, particularly in their careers. Employees who are Type A individuals are passionate perfectionists in their work.[54] Individuals with these distinct personalities are generally *"more successful in [their] work accomplishments."*[55] They create both short-term and long-term goals and work hard to achieve them no matter the phase of life. They are ambitious and have good work ethics, mostly because of their abilities to multitask. They will stay late after work to ensure all tasks are completed and confirm the following day's itinerary. They usually do not require encouragement from their supervisors as they are very self-motivated and cognizant of their obligations. They often take pride in their work because they know they have performed to the highest level. Their superiors also seek them when a job has a deadline because of their dependability. It is, however, unfortunate that those who are Type A *"center their life on their careers"* and may believe that their role in the workplace is *"their [only] purpose in life."*[56]

Nonetheless, can you imagine your life if you applied these same principles in your Christian walk—as if it was your *only* purpose in life? Are we centering our lives to be the best Christians in the field? Is our main purpose in life to share the Good News with everyone around us? Imagine the impact Type A Christians could have on the world if we performed as well in our ministries as we do in our occupations? What if more Type A Christians worked in the ministry field or missions—do you think we could improve the church's overall mission? I know if I were to put as much focus and attention on my church as I do on my career, I would be a more productive Christian in furthering God's Kingdom.

Do you remember how good it felt to actually fulfill a goal in which you had worked so hard to complete, maybe finishing college or paying off your mortgage? Now imagine that same sense of accomplishment when working for the Lord. There are so many individuals on this earth who have such amazing Type A qualities, but only when their passion for Christ exceeds their passion for their careers will their overall goals change to further God's Kingdom.

Sometimes it may be even more difficult to serve the church after working in the corporate world as a leader. While there are many similar qualities when serving in either capacity, serving in a church requires a common goal and doesn't necessitate an actual power of authority—because *Jesus* serves as our intercessor to God, *not* a boardroom full of men or women in suits. Furthermore, we tend to focus on the larger details in our lives and lose sight of the trivial things that actually show us the way in which we should go.

Imagine the Pharisees who knew the Law but missed all the small details and prophecies of our Lord and Savior Jesus Christ. They demanded that Jesus be crucified because they didn't pay attention to the details. Sometimes we have to take a break from our own conscience and listen to that still, small voice (I Kings 19:12). In quoting a recent movie, *Finding Normal*, many of us are *"looking for a god who shouts and completely misse[s] the One who whispers!"*[57] God will use believers who pay attention to His voice and will help them accomplish His tasks and goals. Remember, as Christians, we are offered God's grace, but we will be judged on the opportunities that were provided to us and how we responded to them. It's time to prioritize God's mission over personal goals because seeking the small details will plant seeds, which will lead others to deliverance rather than eternal condemnation.

BENEFITS OF A TYPE A FAMILY MEMBER

Boys and girls with Type A personalities do eventually grow and mature. They have learned the value of working hard and understand the determination it takes to reach a goal, whether it's to become the next CEO or to start a family. Prior to marriage, those who identify with having a Type A personality are often very dependable and responsible. They too understand the value of hard work and never want to disappoint anyone because of their personal limitations or failures. They excel in working under time constraints as they can complete many tasks in a quick and timely manner. Most are very practical with their finances due to a strict budget as they know exactly where to allocate their hard-earned money. And, for those who attend church, they have a great opportunity to serve in the community as they ensure each plan for evangelism is put into action. They may also enjoy teaching a Bible class, serving as a mentor to a youth member, scheduling events and activities, or even serving on the finance committee.

For those who are married, if one spouse is Type A, there may be some difficulty in the marriage, but if both the husband and wife have Type A personalities, the struggle for power may be a large obstacle within the marriage and home. Thankfully, there is clear biblical instruction regarding marriage, and the principles for running a home are attainable for individuals with various personality types.

My husband and I attended our annual weekend marriage retreat hosted by our church in 2016, which was led by Jason and Paige Dees who are friends of our church family. They provide pastoral and counseling services at their home church in Georgia and developed a biblical outline for the following marriage principles.[58]

We learned that in order to have a successful marriage, you must have a chief executive officer or *"CEO"* (the husband) and a *"manager"* (the wife). The CEO basically functions as the most senior leader or administrator within a typical business. A husband who functions as a CEO over the household serves as a *sacrificial* Christian leader who *consistently* directs his family in a Christian lifestyle by attending church regularly, maintaining a steady job to meet the needs of the family, ensuring appropriate tithing, and upholding the fruit of the Spirit in his actions, behavior, and personality. For if he does not provide for his family, then he has *"denied the faith and is worse than an unbeliever"* (I Timothy 5:8). On the other hand, the wife, or the manager, is to run the household similar to a manager within a business. The roles of the wife are to ensure a loving Christian environment while caring for the family, supervising daily functions within the home, maintaining cleanliness, caring for the children, and organizing meals.

Now before you say, wait, what? *Cook and clean?* Obviously, I am a working Type A wife and mom, but rest assured we also talked about *delegation* at our marriage retreat to a large extent. Every good manager learns how to delegate appropriately, whether it is teaching your child the value of work through chores or by simply paying a cleaning service. I prefer both. I am very blessed to have a marriage where my husband and I share many obligations within the home and in caring for our daughter. We have a marriage built on mutual respect for one another, and despite our few arguments, we try to encourage one another in our Christian walks. I am more Type A in certain aspects of our family and marriage, and my husband is more Type A in others, so I feel that we make a good team.

While there are clear biblical instructions found in the Book of Ephesians, this type of marriage is difficult for non-believers to understand because the man is considered to be the leader (5:23). It is also sometimes challenging to explain, especially when a husband may not be the *best* CEO. However, just as in business, everyone has qualities that they either excel or fail at, and a good leader admits to both. Just as in a marriage, it is important for the husband and wife to clarify the roles or qualities to trade off. For example, the husband may be a better cook than the wife, while the wife may have better budgeting skills.

For families who have two working parents, it is very difficult to run a home, but parents with Type A strive to maintain a strict schedule. Their day-to-day operations typically run smoothly. They enjoy creating calendars with specific lists for each family member as well as a family chore list to ensure the house is maintained. Menus are typically pre-arranged in order to satisfy different palates. Evenings at home are also very scheduled to ensure homework is completed, chores are finished, and bedtime stories are recited.

Similarly, Type A stay-at-home parents are no different. They often have endless task lists and are typically never late to appointments, as their schedules are always listed on their cell phone calendars.[59] They may even volunteer at their children's schools or local hospitals to prevent others from thinking they are lazy because that is a title *no* Type A individual want to be called.[60]

For the organized Christian family, prioritizing is key to maintaining relationships with God. The family who loves God also learns to spend time with Him together in daily prayer and Scripture reading. They can also schedule community service projects and learn the importance of putting service to others above their own needs. Parents can also teach their children how to be selfless by donating clothes and toys to others in need. The Christian family can also involve their children in the finances of the household. It is imperative to teach both younger and older children that *all* financial resources are blessings given from God, as well as the importance of tithing and the management of God's money.

BENEFITS OF A TYPE A CHRISTIAN

Now that we have discussed various examples of how Type A traits can benefit our lives and the lives of others, let's focus on improving our Christian walk as we learn to better utilize our traits. I believe having an attention-to-detail trait is an admirable one as it clarifies what values we hold true. We should always be cognizant of matters that lead us away from time spent with our Heavenly Father, and that is something I struggle with often. I often ask myself if the time spent on my own projects, whether it is decluttering our home or organizing photos, benefits my life as a follower of God. It is essential to utilize our time wisely in our Christian walk as we are not promised tomorrow. God expects a lot from us, but He also supplies our every need, just as He promised.

So, regardless of age, there are many significant qualities in a person who embraces a Type A personality. Our traits are important within our homes, schools, and jobs, and now we'll discover how to transition that same success into becoming effective, fruit-bearing Christians. While the church is made up of many different types of people and personalities, we each have a purpose within the church. When Jesus chose His disciples, He knew they would be the future leaders of His Church. They would need to embody many characteristics to lead others to Christ, but they were also blessed with a very special gift, and guess what, we have it, too—the Holy Spirit.

The Holy Spirit lives in every believer and is present in our lives regardless of any situation. The Holy Spirit is with us at our best and our worst, but we have to learn to listen to that still, small voice within to guide our personalities to become productive and fruitful, especially when it comes to maintaining and growing God's Church. In the first Book of Corinthians, we are told *"now that God has set the members, each one of them, in the body just as He pleased"* (12:18). We should be encouraged to be role models within the church and to fulfill our purpose just as Peter told the elders to be examples to others not for dishonest gain or out of compulsion or coercion (I Peter 5:2).

Based upon Type A characteristics, and not being sacrilegious in anyway, we could perhaps say that we serve a Type A God as He is always in control, precise in planning, and demands obedience from His followers. However, Jesus, (i.e. God in flesh), did *not* portray typical Type A behavior in His thinking or actions. As the professed Son of God, this is probably one of the reasons why the Sanhedrin had difficulty believing Jesus because He did not demand perfection—just as they required the Jews to follow the law without fault. Jesus was sent by God to truly show His grace, love, and forgiveness, yet He wants us to be good and honor Him in our behaviors.

Just as the woman caught in adultery was saved from being stoned to death, I would much rather be judged by Jesus who is perfect rather than those who sin like myself. The Sanhedrin who crucified Jesus had forgotten they served a God who, in His own words, is *"merciful and gracious, longsuffering, and abounding in goodness and truth, keeping mercy for thousands, forgiving iniquity and transgression and sin..."* (Exodus 34:6-7).

We, as the body of Christ, have been given the Great Commission to preach, baptize, and teach others *"in the name of the Father and of the Son and of the Holy Spirit"* (Matthew 28:19). This Great Commission was intended to begin just after Jesus ascended into Heaven and after the Promise of the Holy Spirit came upon the believers, and was meant to continue throughout the ages (Luke 24:49). The Holy Spirit helps us make decisions, assists in our comprehension of the Word, cultivates our talents, and ensures the maintenance of our fruit just as in the days of Peter and the disciples who started the church. Although the church is slightly different now—ok, a lot different than when Peter began—we still have the same mission in spreading the Gospel, and what better way than uniting the members of the church for God's purpose.

In order to maintain the church, we must use our positive qualities to ensure its success, especially in a time of persecution, even within the country we live in. Basic functioning of a church is very similar to marriage and the organizing of a home. I previously mentioned the analogy of the CEO and manager within a marriage as it is also essential for leadership roles within the church.

Jesus set the example of being a selfless leader. He sacrificed Himself for not only the church, but for all mankind. He set the example of true agape (selfless) love, which allows us to live under grace. We are blessed to have a Father who loves us so much that He has a perfect plan for each of us. Just after Jesus' resurrection, He charged His disciples to continue spreading the Word of God's grace. God knew that Jesus' followers could not start the church alone, so He blessed them with a Helper, or the Holy Spirit, which is God living within us.

Think about that for a minute? Really, think. God is living inside of you! Think of the children's movie *Inside Out*, which depicts the five different emotions that live inside the brain of the main character, Riley.[61] They each fought to control Riley's response to the world around her. If you think about it, God is in our control booth, so to speak, trying to direct where we go and what we do. We just need to be receptive to His voice and obedient to His directions. He knows when we face danger, He knows when we hurt, and He knows when we are afraid. We should be even more gracious in realizing He understood our need for a Helper during these times, just like those starting the early church. And, no matter what personality traits we possess, we can be certain that God will develop our traits into fruit as led by the Holy Spirit.

Peter and the other disciples were able to complete their mission of spreading God's Word even unto their deaths because they received the promise of the Holy Spirit. Peter also set the tone as a leader within the church for us as believers. The Bible tells us that the beginning of the church was based upon many sacrifices of people who believed in the disciples' message, not to mention those who were already witnesses to Jesus' miracles prior to His death. There were many people who donated everything they owned for the church and its members to flourish (Acts 4:34-35). We must continue to do the same by sacrificing our time to serve others in order to show the love of Christ.

In most instances, the preacher is the leader of the church and congregation, as long as the pastor meets the requirements set out in the New Testament. And, just as the Book of Timothy discusses the requirements of deacons, the church generally consists of leaders who assist with the current overall functioning of the church, which may include assistance with church bylaws, budget, evangelical missions, committees, activities, and perhaps voting on important issues such as purchases within the church, decisions for building renovations, and even materials for Sunday school and worship teams. Perhaps the biggest need for deacons and elders is to take the place of the pastor in cases of absence or sickness, as well as serving as role models for the entire congregation and communities.

There are so many needs within the members of any given church, and it is difficult for one person to meet all of those needs. For example, the first Book of Timothy tells us to care for the widows and elderly in particular, but there are so many other needs. We are told that *"if one member suffers, all the members suffer with it"* (I Corinthians 12:26).

This is where Type A Christians come into play.

The pastor should feel comfortable in delegating roles to those in leadership positions, as well as those who are Type A who welcome tasks in serving others. It also encourages the pastor that he can entrust us to fulfill these roles without having to worry they will not get completed. For those with Type A tendencies, we often think five minutes, five hours, and even five months ahead of others, which makes us successful in maintaining organization for any church. Our pastor can fully rely on those with Type A personalities to carry out tasks in planning and rest assured that every detail has been acknowledged—sometimes twice!

Often those with Type A personalities are considered arrogant and self-absorbed because of certain behaviors toward others; however, the perception that others may have of us is truly important because it can affect the way many feel about the actual Church. Most people do not consider us to be team players[62] due to the fact that some individuals with Type A seem to act superior when we tend to see the worst in others rather than how Jesus sees them.[63] As Type A members, we should always seek ways to edify others within the church, especially offering relief to those in leadership roles without approaching them in a negative way or making them feel that we can do better. We should never feel that way towards others, especially at church. Instead, we should learn to grow or mold these characteristics into features of selfless roles to ensure our personality traits are utilized to the best of our abilities. We should also be thankful and continually pray for other Christians who assist with important decisions relating to the church and in our service to further God's Kingdom.

Type A Christians should never judge others for their iniquities because we are most likely committing a similar sin or behavior, as we can use our past as great witnessing tools. We also need to appreciate the differences of those within the church who may be blessed with more wisdom, faith, healing, etc. It is true that most with Type A personalities are talkers rather than listeners because we typically don't feel the need to listen to other's opinions and may cut them off during a conversation.[64] Hence, we should always enhance the confidence of others in the congregation as they communicate ideas to improve the church. It is always important to include other members when making significant decisions about the church; however, Type A congregation members should also learn to let others lead and carry out tasks within the church rather than feeling the need to control every item or agenda.

In the past, I have often left conversations feeling guilty after a church service or even after speaking to someone from the past because I only answered questions about myself and my family. I wished I would have asked questions to learn more about them. Learning to listen is a true art, and the Book of Proverbs warns us that *"fools find no pleasure in understanding but delight in airing their own opinions"* (18:2). The same book also states those who are listeners are full of knowledge and understanding (Proverbs 17:27).

I feel that becoming a nurse practitioner has allowed me to be a better listener and to ask open-ended questions rather than seeking a simple yes-or-no answer. Regrettably, as a congregation, we often do not spend time asking open-ended questions at church, and a lack of communication is where most churches have disputes. It is the priority of the church to hold Christ at the center and to not lose focus on the mission we have, which is to love God first and *all* others second (Matthew 22:37-39).

We should not be concerned with worldly views of how we dress or look. We should always make guests feel welcomed and comfortable in any Christian church without judgment for being different. Christians, including myself, are sometimes classified as *"hypocrites"* from many who do not attend church. And while there are those within the church who are often just *"filling a seat,"* we are human just like the rest of the world, except we have accepted God's grace. Therefore, as Type A church members, we should desire to learn more about the people God has put in our lives rather than asking basic yes-or-no questions. For crying out loud, we are a *family* of believers! It is essential for others to know we truly care about them and that we place value on their needs above our own—only then can we show self-sacrificial love. You might be surprised how God will use you to become a solution to someone's needs. But first, you must be a willing vessel and then respond as He provides each opportunity.

I have learned through my own small church that we have so many families in different seasons of life, and each of us works for the Lord in various ways. This ensures the functions and roles of the Church are carried out for God's specific purpose and not our own. If engaging others into Christianity is our life purpose, then we should be excited to work with others who share the same faith, even in our differences.

UTILIZING YOUR PERSONALITY

So for those of you who want to transform your personalities but not lose the essence of your talented spirits, I am excited to share with you how to use our opposing Type A traits for God's purpose. This will better illustrate how we can improve ourselves as Type A Christians without completely changing our personalities.

And guess what, as a Christian, you will learn when it's ok to become easily angered, over-burdened, aggressive, impatient, inconsiderate, self-centered, confrontational, self-reliant, and impulsive. That's right! Keep reading to see why the Bible actually approves of these so-called negative behaviors. For a quick review, please note the comparisons between the fruit of the Spirit (Galatians 5:22-23) and Type A traits as mentioned in the first chapter:

FRUIT	**TYPE A TRAITS**
1. Love	1. Easily Angered
2. Joy	2. Over-burdened
3. Peace	3. Aggressive
4. Patience	4. Sense of Urgency
5. Kindness	5. Inconsiderate
6. Goodness	6. Self-centered
7. Meekness	7. Confrontational
8. Faithfulness	8. Self-reliant
9. Self-control	9. Impulsive

LOVE

Now, the first fruit mentioned in the Book of Galatians is love. It's difficult to show love when raging Type A's are quick to anger, especially when someone tells them they are wrong. However, we are encouraged to become angry when anything goes against God's Word and to come to His defense. In fact, Peter tells us to *"sanctify the Lord God in your hearts, and always be ready to give a defense to everyone who asks you a reason for the hope that is in you"* (I Peter 3:15). Just as Jesus became angry in the temple (Matthew 21:12-13), we have an opportunity to demonstrate righteousness through our behaviors when we encounter those who are sacrilegious.

JOY

Our second fruit to bear is joy. Sure, it's easy to be joyful when things go our way, but it's difficult to acknowledge the good when we lead such busy lives. Type A's often work without rest and become easily fatigued. If we are going to be over-burdened, then we should over-commit our schedules for God's work. *"Let us not grow weary while doing good, for in due season we shall reap if we do not lose heart"* (Galatians 6:9). Remember, our diligence on earth is not always rewarded with a paycheck, but we will inherit eternal rewards for all of our good works.

PEACE

The third fruit is peace. While Type A's are typically competitive in nature, we can use this fruit for God's benefit when we are aggressive in our efforts of spreading the Gospel, regardless of our tribulations. We are taught *"do not be ashamed of the testimony of our Lord,... but share with me in the sufferings for the gospel according to the power of God, who has saved us and called us with a holy calling, not according to our works, but according to His own purpose and grace which was given to us in Christ Jesus before time began"* (II Timothy 1:8-9). Avoiding confrontation and keeping the peace is a fruit that many are blessed to display; however, by being aggressive in our desires for doing God's will, Type A's can unite with various personalities to spread the Gospel.

PATIENCE

The fourth fruit is patience. It doesn't take a rocket scientist to understand that we all face times of impatience, which often brings out the worst in each of us. However, we as Type A Christians must use our sense of urgency to the fullest extent when bringing others to Christ. While we understand our time is limited, *"for now our salvation is nearer than when we first believed"* (Romans 13:11). We must always maintain our sense of urgency in providing our testimonies in order to lead others to Christ.

KINDNESS

The fifth fruit is kindness, which leads us to our next Type A trait of being inconsiderate. This is possibly a trait we don't actually see in ourselves, but that we view in others who demonstrate it so well. How can we be inconsiderate to others in a positive way? How about interrupting when they speak? Yes, I said *interrupt*! Interrupt them and tell of God's love when they complain about their hopelessness and despair. The Book of Romans tells us that *"nor height nor depth, nor any other created thing, shall be able to separate us from the love of God which is in Christ Jesus our Lord"* (Ch. 8:39). Both believers and non-believers face times of tribulation, but we must rise above and cast our fears and anxieties to our Creator (I Peter 5:7).

GOODNESS

The next fruit is goodness. Goodness is found in all people, whether believers or non-believers. However, we all become self-centered at times by wanting only the best for ourselves, but we are only at our best when we fully submit to God by learning more about Him. No one else can grow your relationship with God, only you. Learning to be self-centered in growing your relationship with God allows you to avoid the negative influences in your life that may distract you in your walk. We must always *"present [our] bodies a living sacrifice, holy, acceptable to God, which is your reasonable service. And do not be conformed to this world, but be transformed by the renewing of your mind that you may prove what is that good and acceptable perfect will of God"* (Romans 12:1-2).

MEEKNESS

The seventh fruit is meekness. Most of us believe that in order to become meek, we must become weak, which is totally untrue and definitely not a virtue of a Type A individual. We must first learn to be submissive followers of God. However, Type A's have difficulty in submitting to authority, so don't.

Don't submit...to the devil or his corrupt ways! The Book of Ephesians tells us to *"take up the whole armor of God, that you may be able to withstand in the evil day, and having done all, to stand"* (6:13). Remember, we have a roaring lion living inside of us—*"if God is for us, who can be against us?"* (Romans 8:31). Last time I checked, a lion has never been described as meek.

FAITHFULNESS

The eighth fruit is faithfulness. This is the very essence of our belief in Christianity that Jesus Christ, the Son of the Living God, was born of a virgin, sentenced to die on the cross for all sinners, and was resurrected that we may receive eternal life. Unfortunately, individuals with Type A personalities want to have all the answers. We like making decisions after utilizing our knowledge and intellect until we have a concrete answer. However, our self-reliance gets us into trouble from time-to-time. There is a time when it's acceptable to be self-reliant, and that is in our knowledge of the Bible. We must become self-reliant in reading the Word and conversing with God through prayer as we understand *"faith comes by hearing, and hearing by the word of God"* (Romans 10:17). We are also encouraged to be bold in our faith as we uncover the Gospel mystery for non-believers (Ephesians 6:19).

SELF-CONTROL

And, finally, the last of the fruit is self-control. This fruit has caused me distress several times. As I have become fluent in my Type A traits, I have learned (and possibly my husband has suggested) that I can be impulsive in my thoughts and speech (okay, and maybe in my online purchases). However, if we are going to be impulsive in our Christian walk, then let us use this trait in serving and praying for others. We must listen to the Holy Spirit who guides us in being righteous as we display *all* of the righteous fruit. The Book of James tells us that if we know what is good and do not do it, then we are actually committing a sin (4:17). That's right, our lack of displaying these nine attributes will not only cause us to sin against God, but may also hinder others from knowing Christ. So be impulsive. Tell others about Christ. Ask to pray with someone over the phone. Call and ask someone if they need groceries. Send your pastor a note of thanksgiving. All you have to do is ask the Holy Spirit to take control, be impulsive, and good things will happen.

For those of us who are affected with living life as Type A, we should feel proud and honored that God created us for a specific purpose. Teachers love enthusiastic children who want to learn and make good grades. Sports fans love to watch athletes of all ages winning games and making great plays. Children and spouses respect and admire the parent/spouse who has groceries in the fridge, dinner on the table, and clothes laid out for the following day. Co-workers love fellow employees who work tireless hours for others, ensuring goals are met and raises are granted. And preachers love members of the church who complete tasks in a timely manner.

While we may speculate about our purpose in having a Type A personality, we are *still* the *"temple of God,"* and we should continually pray the Holy Spirit who dwells within believers will guide us in producing our best fruit to further God's Kingdom (I Corinthians 3:16). However, it is essential to understand our personalities in how we interact as well as how our actions are viewed by others. In order for us to be effective Christians, whether at home, work, school, church or in the mission field, Type A Christians should recognize that while our worldly personalities are sometimes viewed as arrogant, our goal is to utilize our positive Type A traits as we interact with others to sincerely show Christ-like, agape love and embrace the opportunities as they are provided.

In the following chapter, we will learn about potential, serious consequences for individuals with Type A personalities who do not elicit help from the Holy Spirit to improve their behaviors. By maintaining negative Type A traits, detrimental health risks may occur from persistent stress, which can weaken our abilities to utilize and mature our fruit. Thus, we may never enjoy potential blessings that could impact us and those around us.

CHAPTER FOUR
TYPE A PERSONALITY HEALTH RISKS & COPING STRATEGIES

There are various scriptures written in the Bible on health and how it is affected by one's behaviors, choices, and obedience to God. The Bible even mentions that those who are submissive to His Word will have their lives extended while the lives of those who are wicked will be shortened (Proverbs 10:27-29). Even though we proclaim Jesus as our Savior, our Type A personalities often produce never-ending lists that seem to weaken our bodies until we feel stressed, fatigued, depressed, and guilt-stricken.

In this chapter, we will discuss various health risks associated with Type A personalities, including both physical and psychological effects of chronic stress. Not all who are Type A confront daily stress, and those who do may cope better than others. We all encounter certain levels of stress within our lifetime—some are the consequences based upon our own choices, while others are out of our control. You know what I'm talking about: those unexpected stressors that make you question God's will for your life. Have you ever stopped to think about the *actual* creator of stress? The answer might surprise you. Regardless, it is essential to pray and trust in God as He helps us deal with various stressors by providing coping strategies no matter the origin. As we continue, we will also learn ways to prevent stress in our Type A children.

As a health care provider, I am especially excited to include this chapter. Sometimes information regarding specific health risks can be complicated, so I have written this chapter for easy comprehension on how we are inflicting sometimes irreversible bodily harm. Throughout my years of working in health care, I have learned the importance of listening to my patients to better understand their struggles. I feel this valuable skill helps me avoid similar stressors in my own life and in assessing others at risk during stressful situations.

My husband purchased a wonderful woman's study Bible for my birthday many years ago. It was my first study Bible with reference guides on how to apply biblical topics in my life. As I worked through it, the topic of *"busyness"* caught my eye. My study Bible states that *"busyness is not necessarily godliness"* as it discusses the importance of resisting temptations in over-committing our tasks and schedules.[65] Jesus taught Martha, as well as the rest of us who have an *"action-orient-*

ed personality," to *"abide in Him first, before 'doing' for His Kingdom."*[66] While Jesus understood Martha's personality better than she did, it didn't mean that Jesus didn't love her any less. Jesus also understands each of us and wants us to fully submit to Him before we exercise our fruit. It is an important lesson to learn for all of us—that staying busy for God without true humility only creates unnecessary stress.

We understand the typical Type A individual always keeps busy; however, we should, at the very least, learn to take time to rest after a stressful week from work or home and allow our bodies to heal. When we continue to work and don't allow time to rest, we will undoubtedly become weary. Scripture states *"those who wait on the Lord shall renew their strength ... and not be weary ... and not faint"* (Isaiah 40:31).

We typically don't take the time to recognize the first book of the Bible in Genesis when God, Himself, rested on the seventh day (Genesis 2:2-3). He created the entire universe! And still rested.

So why is resting important, or maybe the better question is, why was rest even mentioned in the early scriptures?

God is telling us to *REST*... not to be lazy, but to rest *after* we work.

We must be patient when life offers choices and pray to God in any decisions to avoid the addition of undesired stress to our lives. When we fail to ask God first, we should be humble in asking Him to help us cope with unexpected outcomes after we have strayed off the path He initially created for us. Now, as we continue reading, let's learn how to improve our current health and well-being by actively avoiding stress.

STRESS AND ITS EFFECT ON OUR BODIES

As the verse in Proverbs says, *"a merry heart does good, like medicine"* (17:22). Well, if this applied to everyone, cardiologists would be out of business, but as we all know, we bring much self-inflicted chaos into our lives and most of us are unaware of the baggage we have created until it's too late. It seems that our hectic daily lives have caused us to lose the joy and peace promised to us as Christians; we don't even realize how stress rules over our lives.

I recently assessed a patient for a routine exam, and during our discussion, we began talking about possible stressors in her life for her complaint of fatigue (which is defined as a state of exhaustion). At first, she denied there were any stressors within the home, family, or even her finances. But five minutes later, she began talking about driving a close family member to her first chemotherapy treatment after her recent cancer diagnosis. My ears immediately perked up. This patient didn't even recognize the amount of stress that her relative's recent cancer diagnosis was causing her.

As a society, we often feel overwhelmed at what we have to accomplish within a given day, week, or month in order to provide and care for our families. This is something we have unfortunately created ourselves—mostly due to our fleshly desires or efforts to keep up with the world. The responsibility in maintaining these standards of living creates an abundance of guilt, which leads to overwhelming stress. This stress can eventually become a chronic condition, which can then trigger various illnesses affecting both physical and emotional states within our bodies. In one of my former nursing textbooks, the writer states *"psychologic stress may cause or [worsen] several disease states, including many of the diseases implicated as leading causes of death in the United States, such as cardiovascular disease and infectious diseases."*[67]

Stress is actually defined as *"the state of affairs arising when a person relates to situations in certain ways"* or *"when a demand exceeds a person's coping abilities, resulting in reactions such as disturbances of cognition, emotion, and behavior that can adversely affect well-being."*[68] In comparison, an online writer describes Type A personality as *"more of a reaction to environmental factors, or tendencies toward certain behaviors and are influenced by culture and job structure."*[69] The writer believes our personalities can be altered or perhaps influenced through *"conscious decisions"* by changing our thought processes into positive thinking, which includes removing the negative stressors or triggers in our lives and by trusting in others.[70]

Conversely, Christians should always involve God when making decisions. When we humbly submit to the Holy Spirit, we can then be transformed from within and avoid many stressors created by listening to the world around us. The process by which we remove negative stressors is following principles found in the Bible and learning to follow God's commands for our lives. Therefore, when we listen to God, we can appreciate His love in helping us avoid stress.

There are two types of stress, which include both real and perceived stressors.[71] *Real stress* is the actual stress on our bodies caused by exercise, thermal changes, and acute emotional stress. *Perceived stress* is anything recognized as stressful or worrisome, such as walking in front of a church congregation to profess Christ as your Savior or perhaps the fear of performing in a church play. Interestingly, both types of stressors—real and perceived—affect different parts of the brain, but can ultimately cause the same symptoms within our bodies. These symptoms include emotional changes in mood and temperament, such as panic attacks as well as increased blood pressure and blood sugar, pupil dilation, piloerection (goose bumps), and increased sweating.[72]

As if sweating and panic attacks aren't enough, individuals living with Type A traits may also experience other various physical characteristics during stress such as facial tension, tight lips, clenched jaw, teeth grinders, dark circles, and facial sweating, which similarly correlates with chronic stress.[73] While these symptoms are difficult to conceal, especially when in public, worrying still produces the aforementioned effects within the body. Dr. David Jeremiah has mentioned on a radio broadcast that 90% of the time the potential situation causing worry never actually happens despite symptoms that persist in our bodies due to stress hormones.[74]

I have thought about his sermon many times when lying down at night to sleep. Many thoughts go through my own head, including our safety through the night, my daughter's safety when she is away from us, safety for my husband while he is teaching at school, my safety at work as well as the safety of my parents and in-laws and other family and friends. I have prayed many times asking God to take over my worrisome thoughts and to take away my stress so that I may rest better. I know that regardless of any situation that may occur, I have a Father in Heaven who loves me as well as my family and friends who are His followers.

STRESSING ABOUT STRESS

There are many books and sermons that discuss the effects of stress and worry on one's Christian walk. The associated symptoms are further clarified by Hans Selye, a Hungarian endocrinologist, who was otherwise known as the *"Father of Stress."*[75] Physiologic stress is important to understand so that we can identify the known reactions our bodies may suffer when faced with stress. Dr. Selye classified three stages within our bodies when dealing with stress, which he titled *General Adaptation Syndrome.*[76]

The first stage is initiated with the onset of stress, or the *"Alarm"* stage, in which our body's awareness or arousal is heightened by stress. This is more commonly called the *"fight or flight"* response. This Alarm stage is marked by an increase in heart rate as well as blood pressure. In addition, glucose is released into the bloodstream to improve energy and focus if needed to *"fight"* or *"flight"* (i.e. run away from) the actual stressor.[77]

The second stage is the *"Adaptation or Resistance"* stage in which our body *"resists and compensates... to return many... functions to normal levels while [the] body focuses resources against the stressor and remains on alert."*[78] It is the intent that our body resumes back to a normal state within minutes or possibly days based on the stressor and our coping skills.[79]

The third stage is *"Exhaustion."* This stage is based upon recurrent stress and signifies the breakdown of our bodies' homeostasis, which is the ability to maintain a condition of stability. Unfortunately, if homeostasis is not renewed, then our bodies are at a greater risk for certain diseases due to a low immune response.[80]

Selye states that recurrent or chronic stress may weaken our immune system and can lead to heart and kidney failure, possibly even death. When we are faced with chronic or daily stressors, our bodies react the same no matter the level of danger. For example, if we were to walk outside and see a slithering snake, our physiological reaction would be just the same as when we arrive at church realizing we forgot to prepare for the communion meditation.[81] This marks an interesting finding from a naturopathic physician who discusses a possible forgotten stage in Selye's stress syndrome, which she has titled the *"Recovery"* stage.[82] For example, random stressors such as hydroplaning in a car may initiate the stress syndrome, and our bodies will hopefully recover and return to normal status quickly. Unfortunately, our state of arousal is unable to detect the difference between an immediate threat like hydroplaning as compared to chronic stress. Losing control of your car on a slick road surface and working a strenuous sixty-hour work week are two very different types of stress, but they can cause the same physiological reaction.[83]

While facing recurrent stress, our stress hormones are persistently being released, and our bodies may suffer both physical and mental effects,[84] which could lead to *"insomnia, anxiety, depression, irritability, and/or emotional instability."*[85] On the other hand, if our bodies face chronic stress, we may suffer severe fatigue, decreased energy as well as poor focus and concentration due to overstimulation and poor compensation by our stress response system.[86]

Based upon Selye's study on the effects of physiologic stress, scientist and Yale professor, John W. Mason, discovered similar findings for psychological stress.[87] He recognized both real and perceived types of stress and defined specific responses.

The first response is *reactive response*. This is where the psychological reaction is based upon an actual psychological stressor, which may be the side effects of a nervous soloist singing for the first time at church or someone arriving for a critical interview with a prestigious employer. Do sweaty palms, dry mouth, nausea, diarrhea, and clammy hands sound familiar? These are all normal hormonal responses from your body when it is exposed to a stressor.

The second response that Mason identified is *anticipatory response*. This response is based on a stressor that is either unfamiliar or possibly from a previous memory, such as when you are visiting a new church, teaching a new Sunday school class, or praying in front of others. Do you feel sweaty, flushed, nauseated, and flustered? Again, these are completely normal responses.

The third response is *conditional response* and is based upon repeated stimuli or stressors. This is a learned response based on recurrent stimuli and may create positive feelings or may generate stress associated with fear or danger. For example, our church provides doughnuts for those who attend Sunday school each week. Initially, young children anticipate doughnuts when they enter the church; however, they become upset when they do not receive the doughnuts on Sunday or Wednesday evenings. As a result of the repeated stimuli (doughnuts), the children have now learned to expect doughnuts only on Sunday mornings.

On the other hand, an undesired and repeated stimulus may induce feelings of fear and danger. Consider someone who may have been the victim of sexual abuse as a child by an authority figure within the church. The child may then associate feelings of fear or danger with each visit to church. These responses may even continue as they age and may hinder the victim from becoming an active member within the church. When some people are faced with these types of extremely stressful situations, they may develop certain phobias and possibly post-traumatic stress disorder (PTSD).[88] Thankfully, these stressful responses may diminish as the negative stimuli lessens. This is a process known as *"extinction"* as the victim continues to attend church and encounters positive experiences.[89]

≈

Facing infertility was one of the greatest stressors I have ever encountered. Yet, when we learned of Reese's hearing loss, my husband and I were devastated—completely astounded and overwhelmed. While we had a great support system in each other and close family and friends, I was quickly reminded of the need to lean on God as my primary source of support.

There were so many times that I could have instantly cried, specifically when other children would ask *why* Reese had to wear hearing aids. Mostly, I cried because I wanted to understand *why* she was born with any disability. The love between my husband and I grew as we served as a source of comfort to each other because no one else could truly understand the struggles we were facing.

I am forever grateful for all the prayers that surrounded my family during those early years, and for those who continue to pray for Reese's future. We are overjoyed by her decision to be a follower of Jesus Christ, and I know that He will continue to protect and bless her during her own Christian walk. We are also extremely blessed to live in the *"Bible belt"* within the United States, where we are able to worship God without extreme persecutions and where church buildings outnumber bars and clubs.

I now understand how fortunate I was to grow up in a two-parent Christian home, and I realize that not everyone has been granted the same blessed upbringing. There are many communities where God is not exalted. There are various cities with residents who face unparalleled stressors while simply walking to school, the grocery store, or to their workplaces. In the United States, many parents' best hope for their children is to graduate high school—a place that should be considered safe, but now gang and criminal involvement dominates and crushes any hopes of attending college. The stressors placed on these parents are incomprehensible to many of us, and we should encourage the promotion of education and safety for all families regardless of any opposition.

Nonetheless, the similarity between various groups of people is that we are all God's creation, and despite our tribulations, we are *"fearfully and wonderfully made"* (Psalm 139:14). As we show praise through reading the Word and daily prayer, we should also maintain obedience to His Word as Proverbs tells us to *"remember His commandments and our days will be lengthened with long life as well as peace"* (3:1-2).

God has given us many promises within the Bible that He will lengthen our days through our humble obedience to Him, as well as our parents (Exodus 20:12). It is written in Deuteronomy that we may live a longer life if we walk in the ways of our Lord and follow His commandments (5:33). When we fail to follow God's instructions, we often suffer the consequences of stress.

The trials we face are most likely caused by our disobedience, which is similar to many characters within the Bible. Learning to trust and obey our Heavenly Father will not only promote a sense of humility and love, but may also lead to the prevention of many self-induced stressors. Above all, we are blessed to have a Savior who came to this earth and suffered death on our behalf, so that we could be fortunate enough to have salvation and live with our Creator forever in Heaven. In return for our obedience, God *will* bless us, maybe not here on earth as we see fit, but in His Kingdom, we will reap His rewards and blessings for an eternity!

SYMPTOMS OF CHRONIC STRESS

Now that we have some background regarding stress, let's discuss the various bodily functions affected by chronic stress. I am confronted at most routine exam visits with questions regarding weight, lack of energy, and symptoms of depression. I know a lot of health care providers face these same questions. While we provide similar recommendations, such as modified diet and exercise, most providers do not truly discuss the many physiological and psychological side effects of stress (or perhaps they do a better job than me).

Unfortunately, there is no magic pill to treat all the various symptoms of stress. And as much as I would love to discuss my patients' relationships with God when helping them with coping strategies, sadly, I must be careful not to overstep boundaries between my job and *"religion."* I do, however, enjoy learning about God's most complex creation—our bodies. Because of this learning, I know we were never meant to work without rest.

It is surprising how symptoms of stress put us at risk for many other health conditions, which negatively affect our body functions over time. Learning how stress affects our bodies is not only vital for those of us with controlling Type A personalities, but also for those who suffer from chronic stress.

While there are many individuals who put forth effort in caring for their bodies through proper nutrition and exercise, sometimes they fail to understand the importance of reducing stress as a part of this regimen. This illustrates the expectations set by God for us to maintain our bodies, not just by the foods we eat (or don't eat), but also in how we maintain mental clarity, which further enables us to produce good fruit. It is important to understand how our actions and behaviors affect our bodies when we try to control our lives by staying busy and not patiently following God's plans. By following Scripture, fearing the Lord, and keeping our bodies ready for His service, we will be righteous and continue to bear fruit as we age (Psalm 94:14).

As previously mentioned, once a stressor is felt or perceived by our bodies, our first response is from our nervous system, which releases stress hormones—adrenaline. When adrenaline is consistently released in times of chronic stress, we are at an increased risk for poor sleep, obesity and high blood pressure.[90]

Another type of hormone released in stressful events is the glucocorticoid hormone, or cortisol. Most women are familiar with this hormone as it is more commonly known as the actual *"stress hormone."* Remember, this is the hormone that leads to our undesired belly fat as well as excess fat in the trunk and face. In addition, it also increases glucose, or blood sugar levels, and may lead to Type 2 Diabetes Mellitus in individuals who deal with chronic stress.[91] See the chart below for specific body systems and their corresponding symptoms of stress.

Body System Effects of Stress[92]

Neuro	Cardio	Respiratory	GI	Endo	MS
Adrenaline →	↑HR ↑BP	↑ Respirations	↑ Blood sugar	↑ Stress hormone	Muscle tension
↓			Nausea	↓	
↑Epinephrine			Vomiting	↑ Cortisol	
↑ Norepinephrine			Diarrhea	(↑ Blood sugar)	
				↓	
				↑ Cytokines	
				↓	
				↑ Inflammation	

Cardiologists Dr. Friedman and Dr. Rosenman were the first to assume patients with Type A personalities suffered with hypertension as well as coronary artery disease (CAD) at a higher rate than individuals who did not possess Type A traits. A diagnosis for hypertension, or elevated blood pressure, is a huge risk factor for developing CAD, which is the main cause of heart attacks, especially if left untreated.[93] Those with *"highly reactive personality types,"* such as Type A individuals, live with higher levels of anxiety and stress and are at risk for a quicker progression to hypertension and CAD as well as an increased mortality rate.[94]

The cardiologists' first research article was published in 1959 and noted patients with Type A tendencies had higher levels of adrenaline than those with other personality types, specifically

Type B.[95] Remember, patients were medically diagnosed with Type A personalities if they met five of the nine criteria or characteristics. While we understand that not all the characteristics may lead to an increase in blood pressure, it was documented that characteristics such as *"urgency, impatience, anger, and hostility, are responsible for the increased risk."*[96]

There have been many studies following the work by Dr. Friedman and Dr. Rosenman, which led the National Heart, Lung, and Blood Institute to include Type A behavior as one of the risk factors for developing cardiovascular disease.[97] One study published in 2012 showed that one-third of Type A individuals suffered with heart disease.[98]

Please see the following table for a detailed list of various symptoms and illnesses imposed on the body in relation to chronic stress.

Chronic Stress Effects To The Body[99,100]

Neuro	Cardio	Respiratory	GI	Endo	MS
Headaches	Heart Attacks	Airway Constriction	Diabetes	Diabetes	Muscle Fatigue
Migraines	Strokes	(COPD/ Asthma)	Gastric Ulcers	Obesity	Headaches
Nausea	Irregular HR	Panic Attacks	Nausea	Lung Disease	Migraines
Vomiting	Hypertension		Vomiting	Heart Disease	Low Back Pain
Light Sensitive	Lack of Energy		Diarrhea	Vascular Disease	
Vision Changes			Irritable Bowel	Strokes	
Sleep Changes			Indigestion	Blood Clots	
Depression				Arthritis	
Poor Focus				Depression	
Sweating				Anxiety	
				Gastric Ulcers	
				Malaise	
				Certain Cancers	

STRESS & DEPRESSION

Finally, as mentioned previously, chronic stress as we all know can lead to chronic mood disorders, including depression. Chronic depression is one of the most common medical diagnoses as it affects 1 in 20 Americans who are twelve years of age and older per Centers for Disease Control and Prevention (CDC) reports during 2009-2012. It is considered more prevalent in females from the ages of 12 to over 60.[101] And, while females report symptoms of depression more often than males in every age category, males report their highest level of depression during the ages of 40-59, which is also the highest age group for females.[102] *"Nearly 90% of persons with severe depression reported difficulty at work, home, or social activities related to their symptoms."* Unfortunately, however, only one-third of these persons actually report seeing a mental health professional in a given year.[103]

Many providers treat depression with prescription medications, mostly because patients come to the office asking for a specific medication that *"works"* for their friend. However, patients do not realize that each of our bodies is completely different, and they may not respond the same to the medications their friend may be taking due to sex, age, weight, health, and genetic make-up, which has been studied through more current genomic testing.

Obviously, the goal of treatment for depression is to decrease the presumed cause of inflammation or to treat the cause of the increased stress hormones, which will be different for everyone. It does not, however, treat or prevent specific stressors or situations that may trigger the depression symptoms. Unfortunately, from my experience, most patients just want to be treated with medication, hence, only a few of my patients consider counseling based upon my recommendation.

Counseling can be beneficial because it allows an individual to talk through his or her difficulties, which may lead to a possible solution rather than taking prescription medication. The combination of counseling with medication can significantly improve depression symptoms. Interestingly, only 50% of individuals have a good response to initial prescription medications, which mainly focus on changing the functions of hormones within the body.[104] One could look at this 50% symptom improvement with a glass half-full or a glass half-empty perspective. However, I presume that while there are various types of prescription treatments that target hormones, most of these individuals are placed in stressful situations daily and are unaware of the dangerous side effects of stress or the role it plays on both physical and psychological health.

Clearly, in any form, stress modification is necessary to decrease our stress hormones from constant activation and will be different for each person. Until we start to look at the actual causes of our presumed depression symptoms, we may never receive a full recovery.

Let's spend some time discussing depression within the scope of Christianity. Despite unanticipated events that may occur within our lives, we as Christians are to be the light for others to see in this world of darkness. Sometimes, when our experiences evoke feelings of sadness, our light may temporarily dim, but we should never lose our faith in God as He will help us over time to shine our lights even brighter than before. Others should also be able to look to us for hope as we share that in spite of our personal trials on earth, we have a Heavenly Father who loves us even when we feel alone.

Through my husband's coaching career, we have been introduced to many families. One of these families depicts this analogy very well. Terry is the announcer for most of the high school athletic events and does a wonderful job with an overwhelming sense of enthusiasm and humor. My daughter adores him as we frequently visit the press box during many cold, spring baseball games. I don't know how, but he never misses a play despite their conversations in the box about ponies, cartoons, and favorite foods. My husband has also developed a wonderful friendship with him through the years, and they have recently encouraged each other when delivering sermons at their respective home churches.

Many years ago, Terry sadly lost his brother, Phil, to cancer. A few years later, Terry and his wife, Tammy, lost their youngest son, Josh, who was eight years old, to a rare genetic disease. I did not know them well during that time, but I was at the football field one Friday night in 2010 when members of the team carried Josh onto the field prior to the game—there was not a dry eye in the stands as supporters cheered him on! Just hearing Terry talk about his young son after his passing always brings tears to my eyes because he and his wife and older son, Jake, endured such a long journey with no happy ending... unless you are a Christian. Today, they continue to celebrate

Phil and Josh as they wait to be reunited with them once again in Heaven.

While Terry and Tammy's lights may have dimmed for several years while helping their son fight for his life, they have continued to persevere as Christians in serving others. Along with close friends and family, they created the P.H.I.L. (People Helping In Love) Foundation, named for his brother as a way to help other families suffering with similar health complications (http://www.philfoundation.org/).[105] Their mission acronym is J.O.S.H. in honor of their beloved son, which stands for *"Just Out Serving Him."* They have also organized a wonderful 5K race and mud run in honor of their son titled *"Little Ironman,"* in homage to Josh's love of superheroes. And they continue to exemplify the verse in Matthew used in promotion for their foundation, which states, *"Let your light so shine before men, that they may see your good works and glorify your Father in Heaven"* (5:16). All of the proceeds go to other families facing similar situations. Terry, Tammy, and their family received much assistance from their community, as well as their church, and this is their way of giving back.

The community of Christians who supported this family, as well as others in need, continue to shine their lights as they demonstrate compassion in times of ultimate loneliness. The family who lost their son could have sunk into a state of depression. In fact, today's society would have expected such behavior caused by the sorrow of losing a beloved child. One reason they chose to persevere was the unforgettable smile on their son's face while he was living—not to mention their need in serving as parents to Jake, who also endured the loss of his only brother. In the many pictures and videos of their son, he was always smiling and laughing for the camera. He was a light—one that eventually darkened on earth but continues to shine through the love of others.

After my family participated in the race this past summer, my daughter asked if she and Josh, the son of her favorite announcer, would have been good friends. I quickly nodded and told her I'm sure they would have laughed and played at the baseball games, but as sadness entered its way through tears, I was comforted and continue to be so in knowing that one day they *will* laugh together in the Light of our Lord.

Perhaps the greatest Psalm is the writings of David in chapter 23. The Lord is our Shepherd, He is always leading us, and all that He asks is for us to trust and follow Him. Have you ever thought that God has set us out as shepherds for others, especially during their times of trial and tribulation? When is the last time God gave you an opportunity to be a shepherd for someone? Did you shy away from the chance? Or were you able to provide direction or maybe grace amidst the troubles they were facing? We are all shepherds to many, including those at work, our youth at church, and non-believers we may encounter.

For those of us who have endured circumstances causing depression, whether short-term or long-term, the Bible actually describes us as blessed. The first chapter in James states, *"Blessed is the one who perseveres under trial because, having stood the test, that person will receive the crown of life that the Lord has promised to those who love him"* (1:12). My local church's name, Promise Ministries, indicates that we rightly claim God's promises. A quote my preacher has mentioned in the past is: *"We're not worthy, but God says we're worth it!"* What a testament to God's love for us in that He sent His only Son to die for all of us.

No amount of sadness or depression should ever trump God's love for us, and in return, Jesus only asks that we love God and show love for others. It's hard to be a loving person when depression is consuming us on the inside—sometimes it's easier to hold on than to let go—but that's what God is waiting on you to do. Pray now that you can let go of all the stressors holding you back from living a fuller life. Once you have fully entrusted God with your stressors and worries, only then can you start producing your fruit to the best of your ability.

Stress in Men and Women

As previously stated, Type A personalities are especially prone to stress in all forms. It slowly creeps into our lives unexpectedly and then waits for the most inopportune time to attack. While many with Type A characteristics feel they thrive under stress, they could not be more wrong as proven by the many associated health risks from chronic stress.

Now that we have learned countless ways in which stress affects us physically and mentally, let's look into some of the differences in how body systems differ between men and women. Stress is described as the *"most negative effect on our immunity—*

characterized as uncontrollable, undesirable, and overtaxing the individual's ability to cope."[106] I have faced many stressors in my life that have affected me personally as well as those that I have shared with my husband. I have learned that we both face stress differently.

First, let's discuss the effects of male stress. I will use my spouse as an example. For starters, I love my husband and absolutely hate when he is stressed, especially when there is nothing I can do to minimize it. Most of his stressors are related to his job as a coach. Any coach will tell you that it's not the game but everything else around it that is stressful. He has faced many situations throughout his many years of coaching in dealing with the players, the parents, fundraising, disciplining, etc. Unfortunately, the majority of his stressors involve the parents rather than the players. The typical question is always related to *"playing-time."* Fortunately, the game of baseball is all about statistics. My husband is meticulous when it comes to organizing his players' stats per game and is able to provide the parents with their son's inefficiencies. He tries to make the best decisions for his players every season no matter the struggles within the team. He also understands his role as both a coach and a mentor as he teaches his players discipline on and off the field in preparation for life after high school graduation. Surprisingly, he has had many players approach him and actually apologize for their parents' behaviors or emails (I think because they understand that my husband is a fair coach). However, the stress in being any type of leader comes with a price, and for my husband, he sometimes has a difficult time letting go. This is obvious when he comes home with stress from the field weighing heavy on his mind. Even our daughter can sense his change in mood.

The stress my husband faces is not unique to him. Stress can affect all men. While all boys mature physically during puberty, they may not mature mentally at the same rate. Regardless, at some point boys are finally viewed as grown men. And with that comes certain expectations. Younger men may not attend college because they are caring for younger siblings, especially if they are from a single-parent home. Perhaps they are pressured to take on the family business. Young husbands and fathers discover new stressors in caring for their own families as they may not have had Christian fathers to teach them how to be leaders of their families. Later, older men may face serious job concerns including lay-offs from companies where they have worked for many decades, which can lead to an overwhelming amount of stress, especially at a time nearing retirement. Stress at any age is detrimental, and men, especially, face serious consequences.

When a male is triggered by his stress response syndrome, he produces testosterone that initiates adrenaline.[107] If the *"stress hormone"* or cortisol level is increased by recurrent stress, this may weaken the male's reproductive response. So apparently, for those of us dealing with infertility, it may not be beneficial to constantly ask about the health of your husband's sperm.

See the following table for effects of stress specifically on men and their hormones. This is in addition to the general effects shown above that affect both genders.

Effects Of Stress in Men[108]

↑ Adrenaline	↑ Cortisol	↑ Testosterone	↓ Reproductive Response
Altered testosterone, decreased sperm production, erectile dysfunction, risk of infection to testes and prostate			

Stress was actually mentioned in the Book of Exodus when Moses' father-in-law was explaining the importance of delegation. He warned Moses that if he did not choose God-fearing men to listen to the Israelites, then he would suffer exhaustion and would most likely neglect his role as leader (Exodus 18). This is an early example suggesting the man of the household should have Christian friends and co-workers to provide guidance and moral support, not to mention a respectful spouse and children. God has created us with individual talents, and in order to prevent a state of burden, we were meant to work together, not against each other. When we compare ourselves with one another, our competitive nature shouldn't overrule our Christian faith or our relationships with fellow believers—this includes females as well.

Most men, in general, do not like others telling them what to do, particularly females and especially if it is in relation to fixing a car or giving directions. Most men with Type A possess competitive temperaments and are usually last in congratulating someone who has reached the same goal first. Regrettably, this may lead to jealous tendencies, especially in close family units or with co-workers, and can lead to low self-esteem issues as well as internal stress. This is especially true when other individuals are succeeding at a time when Type A individuals are not.

Therefore, Christian men should always give positive feedback without being overly critical. Sometimes, we often show more compassion to strangers than our own family, and this is something that must start at home and then trickle into our churches and work settings. At times, men have trouble showing emotions, but the Bible tells us to *"rejoice with those who rejoice, and weep with those who weep"* (Romans 12:15). Dr. Jeremiah suggests that Christians usually do a pretty good job of empathizing and offering support to others when they are down or in need, but not so good in rejoicing or offering praise when others are successful.

The American Psychological Association agrees that men, in general, do not like to discuss any physical or emotional symptoms of stress. However, 76% of men report their work as the main cause of stress.[109] Men also have a greater responsibility in their role as head of the family and may feel inadequate if they are not serving as a good husband or provider. Unfortunately, a mere 30% of men report they are successful at managing stress, which implies 70% either have poor coping skills or no coping skills at all.[110] In the same article, only 18% of men report going to church or *"religious services"* as a means to manage stress (compared to only 27% of women), and an astounding 43% of men believe an increase in money will decrease stress.[111] However, coping skills utilized most by men include exercise, playing sports, and listening to music.[112]

We'll discuss coping shortly, but next, let's talk about stress and its effect on women.

Over the last half-century, women of all ages have faced common stressors, mostly because of the extra workload we have created for ourselves. Young female students try to fit in with the world around them as they develop and maintain self-esteem. As this happens, teenage girls encounter stressors such as body image issues and the like. Young women try to keep up with young men in college and hope to be considered for interviews and positions similar to males. Women are constantly making difficult decisions while balancing a family and career. Later, older females are adjusting to empty nests and other common stressors such as retirement and financial concerns, various health issues, and learning to care for elderly parents or possibly a spouse in poor health. Women in menopause also face multiple hormonal changes, and depending upon her coping skills, *"the change"* may lead to undesirable symptoms affecting both the woman and her family.

It is difficult for me to offer advice to women at certain times in their lives when I am not currently affected by similar stressors. But most coping strategies are universal. This is why it is important to learn how to cope at a young age and to maintain our faith and trust in God as He guides us through both natural and unexpected events in our lives. In my role as a nurse, I often talk with patients about commitments and overloaded schedules, our relationships and roles as wives and mothers, and our responsibilities at work and as caretakers for either children or aging parents. I also talk about our lack of proper nutrition and exercise.

I can personally empathize with many of my patients in regards to being a working mother and wife. In 2013, 70.3% of women with children under the age of 18 were in the workforce, compared with 47.4% in 1975.[113] It is very challenging to go to work and then come home to clean, cook, and help with homework—all while trying to find time to exercise. I realize that I am very lucky to have a wonderful husband who assists with all of the above, but sometimes, I am just too tired to exercise. I have noticed a difference in women who make an effort to exercise; they are very proactive in making changes that promote health. I frequently advise my younger patients to ensure health is a priority and to encourage self-discipline prior to marriage and starting a family because we all know our time is very limited when the kiddos come along.

So let's look at the processes that stress causes on our female bodies. See the table below for a list of female hormones and altered effects caused by stress.

Effects Of Stress in Women[114]

↑ Adrenaline	↑ Cortisol	↓ Testosterone	↓ Luteinizing Hormone
↓ Thyroid Hormone	↓ Progesterone	↓ Growth Hormone	↑ Prolactin
Irregular menses, mood changes, eating disorders, anxiety, depression, poor sleep, weight changes, decreased sexual desire, autoimmune/ inflammatory diseases, premenstrual syndrome			

Women who do not learn to cope with stress may also be at risk for enhanced PMS, or premenstrual syndrome. This may lead to a significant drop in daily activities with friends and family or may cause frequent absences at work.[115] Affected relationships often include one's spouse, family, and closest friends. Stress plays a significant role in our response time, our energy levels, and in how we feel about ourselves.

As women with Type A, our time to rest is infrequent due to our hectic schedules. When we do not allow our friends or families to help us, then we are only straying from those who love us. Our spouse should serve as a loving support system, which is why God created marriage in the first place because He desires us to have intimate relationships with each other. When we miss out on intimacy with our spouse, our relationship may struggle and this could lead to significant stress within the marriage.

Remember, stress remains heavily concealed at times, and we don't recognize it until it has caused irreversible damage. In realizing that stress may occur without anticipation, it is crucial to recognize stressors that can be quickly eliminated solely based upon the choices we make. So how do we recognize the stress that we need to avoid? First, we must understand where stress actually originates.

WHO IS THE CREATOR OF STRESS?

We have talked about the definition and various types of stress, and hopefully you now have an understanding of the many side effects produced by chronic stress. Several treatments have also been mentioned, but none have actually been shown to prevent stressors. It's not until we understand where stress originates that we will understand how to initially prevent stress. You might find the answer surprising because there is only one who is responsible for these stressors, and if you are waiting to read, *"It's you,"* then you're actually wrong.

It's none other than... *Satan*!

Actually, he is the responsible party for *all* our negative stressors, and everything that takes our focus away—discrediting our faith in our Heavenly Father. Satan first created stress, worry, and anxiety through Adam and Eve when he caused separation between God and His creations. Eve demonstrated free will as she took the bite of the forbidden fruit, but it was Satan who led her astray from the will of God. Sin was introduced in the garden that day, and our bodies have suffered the consequences since that time. Satan understands the havoc that stress can cause. He disguises himself in many different realms, but no one ever stops to realize he is the one who desires our lives to become unraveled, not God.

Satan also understands the demand for obedience, as this is one of the reasons he was thrown out of Heaven. He is keenly aware that God's people will face tribulations when we disobey and follow our fleshly desires (Deuteronomy 28:15). In the Book of Deuteronomy, there are *14* verses that discuss God's blessings upon us when we obey Him compared to *53* verses regarding the many curses for our disobedience (Ch. 28). The devil provides us with many fleshly incentives *not* to follow

God, like power, wealth, and lusts (2 Tim 3:4), but he cannot promise eternal salvation.

It's true that God gave us free will to choose and make decisions in all parts of our lives, but God doesn't want us to live a life full of stress and worry. Unfortunately, the devil wants us to endure a constant state of stress so we don't even recognize when he is attacking. Therefore, we should pray daily for the Holy Spirit to intervene as we make the decision to be productive instead of destructive. The Book of Proverbs also states, *"do not overwork to be rich"* (23:4). We truly need to sit back and understand the purpose of our job. Is it to gain wealth, prestige, and material possessions alone (which produces stress with its many side effects)? Or is it to glorify God and provide for our families?

We do not always have control over the stress that enters our lives, but it is how we react that is important. As Paul spoke in the Book of Romans, Christians are not exempt from stress and tribulations, but *"tribulation produces perseverance, and perseverance, character, and character, hope"* (Romans 5:3-4). We all have deadlines at work or at school, and we all face unforeseen events. Life is not always going to go as planned; it is important to realize all of God's plans are perfectly designed, and we must persevere. Just as God is quick to forgive, He will help us cope with stress when we fail, as long as we display humility in expressing our need for His guidance.

COPING WITH STRESS

The first step in learning how to cope is to ask God to declutter the stress in our lives. The Bible tells us *"[d]o not be wise in [our] own eyes; Fear the Lord and depart from evil. It will be health to your flesh, and strength to your bones"* (Proverbs 3:7-8). Stress comes from many different avenues, including our health, relationships, work, studies, finances, and sometimes church. And let's not forget about the worry, fear, shame, and guilt that stress often brings. Often we become so distracted in our lives that we don't stop to realize what's important. Proverbs tells us to *"commit your works to the Lord, and He will establish your plans"* (16:3). God knows our desires, but when we don't include Him, the path for our lives will most likely lead to stress and possibly destruction.

Fortunately, we have the promise of a Helper when we need to make difficult decisions in our lives. Jesus tells us in the Book of John that if we love Him and keep His Word, then God will love us, and in turn, will grant us the promised Helper or Holy Spirit (14:23, 26). Many agree that our conscience serves as our moral sense or intuition, which guides us in deciding between what is right and wrong; I passionately disagree! As Christians, we understand that the Holy Spirit is part of the Trinity—God (the Father), Jesus (the Son), and the Holy Spirit—who lives within each Christian who has accepted Jesus as their personal Savior.

The Holy Spirit is much more than our inner self speaking to us, it is the actual Spirit of God (I Corinthians 3:16). The first Book of Corinthians tells us the body is the temple of the

Holy Spirit, and we are to glorify God in our body and in our spirit because we were *"bought at a price"* through the blood of Jesus Christ (6:19-20). While we have the same Holy Spirit that dwelled within Jesus Christ and helped Him resist temptation, it is essential to recognize the power of God in Spirit and have faith that He will provide us wisdom in our time of need.

The Holy Spirit not only guides our conscience in our thoughts and personalities but also serves as the distributor of our spiritual gifts as well as our intercessor when we pray to God. I could never assume any spiritual gift or decision I make is based upon my own actions or conscience. We must always give credit to the Holy Spirit who guides us in our Christian walk.

Jesus spoke, *"Peace I leave with you, My peace I give to you; not as the world gives do I give you. Let not your heart be troubled, neither let it be afraid"* (John 14:27). While we are promised many gifts from our Father in Heaven, we are also met with many trials on earth, mostly from choices we make, as well as those solely related to the power of sin. When we acknowledge God as our Creator, He can provide for us in ways we never dreamed of, which vastly differs from how we try to satisfy ourselves in a world that boasts personal gain.

Now don't think I am writing this chapter on stress because I have learned how to eliminate it from my life. I wish I had a magic solution for avoiding it, but I am human and suffer from stress just as much as the next person. My Type A personality overbooks my daily schedule, helps my daughter succeed in school and whatever sport she is competing in, assists my husband in editing his graduate papers, feeds and walks the dog, attempts to cook Pinterest-worthy meals, and ensures my home is clean and organized—oh, and don't forget about my full-time job.

As you can see, when our schedule is overbooked, there is not much room for studying the Word, is there?

Over the last few years, I have realized the importance of spending time with God and furthering my relationship with Him. When we finally put God at the top of our priorities, it leaves little room for distractions and helps remove clutter within our lives. When we solely rely on others to teach us about God and not actively participate in forming our own relationships with Him, we may have trouble understanding His guidance. Stress plays a huge part in taking our focus away from God, and that is just what the devil wants to have happen. But even when we have our priorities in order, the devil is ready to attack and throw us off again.

The major causes of stress in my life are probably similar to many others. I worry that my husband and I are not persistently raising our daughter in the way God approves. I worry she may be unprepared to face this cruel world on her own. I worry that I'm not a humble wife to my God-fearing husband. I worry that I am not able to participate in missions due to decreased availability of my time. I worry about whether or not I am adequately taking care of my patients and not letting my co-workers down. I also worry that I am not as healthy as I should be in regards to my diet and exercise, or lack thereof. And I always worry about my family's health and safety.

I understand these are very common anxieties which may produce stress within each of us; however, we have a Savior who tells us, *"do not worry about tomorrow, for tomorrow will worry about its own things. Sufficient for the day is its own trouble"* (Matthew 6:34). We cannot worry and trust in God at the same time. In order to claim God's provisions, we must *"seek first the Kingdom of God and His righteousness, and all these things shall be added unto you"* (Matthew 6:33). It's when we find ourselves completely distracted by the stress in our lives that we need to take a step back and lean on our Heavenly Father and His Helper.

While Satan puts many obstacles in our lives, we should *" [b]e anxious for nothing, but in everything by prayer and supplication, with thanksgiving, let your requests be made known to God, and the peace of God, which surpasses all understanding, will guard your hearts and mind through Jesus Christ"* (Philippians 4:6-7). When we keep our focus on God's will for our lives, we can look past all of the barriers that the devil uses to steer us off God's path. God demands our obedience, yet He is also a forgiving God who rejoices when we ask His forgiveness and direction. This is why it is important to acknowledge the Holy Spirit's guidance through all of life's struggles and tribulations.

In the Book of James, we are told to *"call the elders of the church, and let them pray over [you]"* (James 5:14). Have you ever considered asking for prayers from those at your church for your struggles? While we may be responsible for some items which cause stress, I can guarantee that no one in our churches can completely avoid facing stress within their own lives. Hopefully, you are attending a church that edifies you in your time of need, just as Jesus instructed us to do.

Unfortunately, we have a hard time giving God our worries because we have all the answers, right? Have you ever reached a certain point in your life and wondered how you got there? Sometimes, we think back on life's curves and twists and wonder what we could have done differently. As I reflect back, there are definite changes I would have made in my own life. Fortunately, I was saved at a younger age, but even still I knew I was not behaving as a Christian at certain points in my life. Again, I am thankful for God's gift of grace and mercy, and I am always thankful for the many times I have received His blessings of encouragement and love through others. Thankfully, He has blessed each of us with the ability to cope with many of life's trials through His Word.

Coping is actually defined as the *"process of managing stressful demands and challenges that are praised as taxing or exceeding the resources of the person."*[116] Management of stress may come through positive changes in behavior, such as reading your Bible daily, deepening your prayer life, or joining a social support or counseling group. Other individuals choose to manage stress through negative behaviors by avoidance in relationships, overeating, or maybe through binge-drinking or illicit drug use, which may also lead to depression, poor sleep, and risk for illness.[117]

There are two well-known methods of positive and negative coping behaviors, otherwise known as emotion-focused and problem-focused strategies.[118] Emotion-focused coping strategies suggest the need to change one's emotions when stressors are uncontrollable, unforeseen, or unchangeable.[119] This coping strategy is mostly utilized by females as we often see the positive in many stressful situations and may also seek support through family and friends.[120] For example, a preacher or leader of the church may encourage emotional coping for someone with a new cancer diagnosis or the sudden loss of a spouse or child.

On the other hand, some individuals choose to avoid or ignore the actual stressor, which may truly worsen symptoms of stress. For example, someone who has suffered abuse or had a previous abortion may develop symptoms of guilt, shame, embarrassment, or regret. The internal stress within these individuals may also lead to an overwhelming state of depression. These individuals would greatly benefit from appropriate counseling, as well as recommendations in changes to their coping skills. As followers of Christ, if any individual chooses to share their personal history, we should show encouragement rather than judgment. We should never miss an opportunity to share the Gospel of the One who came to save the earth and not condemn it (John 3:17).

Problem-focused coping strategies are better suited for stressors that can be controlled or minimized through *"problem solving, time-management, [and] obtaining instrumental social support."*[121] Problem-focused coping strategies work well for those who are detail-oriented and who find solutions to resolve stressors. Examples of problem-focused strategies within the church include setting the budget, deciding on missions to pursue, or scheduling of events. While problem-solving may be beneficial for those who are Type A Christians, they may become easily irritated when they attempt to solve issues within the church that cannot be changed.

Either strategy is important in learning how to cope because the devil will not lose focus in trying to distract God's adopted children—no matter the age.

I truly wish we didn't have to face these stressors and suffer with anxiety, but understanding how to cope at a younger age is a valuable lesson on how to rely on God as our Helper. God wants us to come to Him with all of our concerns but also afterwards with thanksgiving. As we become more dependent on God, prayer becomes an excellent coping strategy and teaches us both humility and faithfulness, especially when life doesn't go as planned.

Coping is also important at young ages because as we become physically older, we may face a decline in how our bodies react to stress, as well as a decrease in adaptation and coping skills.[122] It's no wonder the original *"Father of Stress,"* Selye, was quoted as saying that *" [e]very stress leaves an indelible scar, and the organism [or human] pays for its survival after a stressful situation by becoming a little older."*[123] For those parents of teenagers, do you feel like you have aged twice as fast? How about those facing a layoff at work: do you feel that the stress is overwhelming?

One symptom of chronic stress that I can empathize with is migraine headaches. I always thought I was pretty good at coping throughout my nursing career in the emergency department and completing my graduate degree as a nurse practitioner, but one summer my body could cope no more. I had nearly three years of experience as a provider and was transitioning with my supervising physician to another medical facility, as well as preparing for a small home addition. It was during this time, after the completion of our addition and office change that I suffered my first migraine preceded by visual changes. I was told by our local optometrist that migraines usually occur *after* a stressful event has occurred, which meant it probably took my body two to three months to return back to somewhat of a normal state.

I realized that I allowed both situations to take over my life, and my controlling Type A personality did not help me manage every small detail. After suffering my first migraine, I assured myself that I would learn better coping skills and would try to let go of some of the control of any future remodels. I know that I definitely aged a few years during that summer, but we truly enjoy our new family room as well as our new office space and coworkers. It did, however, come at a high cost to my body.

Obviously, men and women handle stress very differently, and there are various techniques and coping strategies, which include both education and relaxation. My husband is a runner and is able to decrease stress by running long-distance. I, on the other hand, want to learn as much as possible regarding the actual stressor, such as my daughter's hearing loss. When Reese was having ear tubes inserted after a decline in her hearing, the surgeon discovered a *cholesteatoma*, which is basically a cyst on the eardrum. We received a call from the surgeon, who was still in the operating room, notifying us of his finding, and my brain immediately thought of cancer since some cancer diagnoses end with the word, *"-oma."* I quickly researched it on my cell phone so that I would have questions ready after the procedure was completed. My husband, on the other hand, who couldn't take a jog around the hospital to release his nervous energy, was very upset at the fear of this unknown finding and continued to pace the floor. All three of us had prayed the night before and the morning of her surgery. This cholesteatoma was actually an answered prayer—we just didn't realize it yet.

From the earliest stages of her hearing diagnosis, we were always told that Reese's hearing could potentially worsen over time because there were no known causes for her hearing loss. Fortunately, we quickly learned that the cyst on her eardrum was actually the cause of her worsened hearing loss. It was God's blessing in disguise that our surgeon was able to discover it during the procedure. She will most likely require a future *"patch"* surgery to her eardrum, but if it had gone undetected, the cholesteatoma may have caused further hearing loss and irreversible damage. By having faith in God, we were able to see His blessings from Reese's surgery that day rather than focus on the possibility of future surgeries.

As we've talked about before, sometimes stress is not something we can control, but we can be exalted when we have faith in a God we can lean on and cast ALL our cares on (1 Peter 5:7). I will never forget talking with the nurse as we walked into the post-operative area to discover Reese was able to hear our conversation *without* her hearing aids! I quickly whispered a very humble and thankful prayer to our Lord that morning. I realized that God is so powerful and makes the unbelievable a reality. I never dreamed there was the possibility of a cyst on Reese's eardrum or that it could be the cause of her hearing loss. Sometimes that's just how life goes. It's only when we truly lose control that we receive God's blessings in ways we never imagined.

Can you think of a time when God surprised you or showed you another way of accomplishing something that you never knew existed on your own?

I can think of several times when I knew God had His hand on me in the past. It was meeting my husband after several years of poor dating experiences. It was the day I tested positive on a pregnancy test at home *without* using fertility medications. It is watching my daughter become independent after years of praying she would *"be okay"* despite her hearing loss. It was attending nurse practitioner school and learning a completely new specialty in obstetrics and gynecology and actually loving it. Now it is becoming more involved with church and learning something new with every reading, every prayer, every sermon, every Bible study, every marriage retreat, and every small group. It is writing this book and realizing how many people God has placed in front of me at just the right time in order to complete the process.

Through prayer and restoration, we can be assured that coping will become easier as we face life's tribulations. It is also vital to understand that some coping strategies may work for some, but not for others. McLeod, a psychologist professor, says that *"coping strategies are just as important as personality."*[124] For example, extroverted individuals with Type A, like myself, are more expressive with our feelings and emotions, while introverts seem to suppress most of their feelings. McLeod also states that not expressing our feelings can actually lead to poor physical health by compromising one's immune system.[125] When I have a stressor that is inevitable, I usually resort to eating chocolate, listening to music, or watching a favorite TV show or movie. It is a valuable tool for individuals with Type A to learn how to manage stress using healthy coping skills rather than adverse effects that may lead to worsened side effects on our bodies.

Coping strategies may also include biofeedback, which is how we control our body functions.[126] Examples of biofeedback include learning to relax muscles and developing other techniques such as how to control breathing, body temperature, heart rate, and sweat glands.[127] Biofeedback can be monitored by many wearable devices, including interactive computers and mobile devices.[128] Other strategies include journaling, which consists of writing about possible triggers and the emotions that stressors activate.[129] Journaling can also identify stressors that cause abnormal or undesired changes in emotions and can provide insight for possible solutions.[130]

Understanding our stressors and coping techniques can help us face fears when confronted by specific triggers and then learn to apply methods for recovery. For example, when my daughter is feeling ill, she becomes more relaxed when she cuddles with me, her dad, or our dog while she rests. On the other hand, my nephew, who is not a fan of animals, would have increased anxiety within close proximity of any dog.

I totally understand his fear. While I feel completely relaxed on a beach vacation, my heart rate immediately spikes when my daughter asks me to get in the ocean with her as I am fearful of pretty much any marine life, specifically sharks. Apparently, repetitive exposure has been shown to improve reactions to certain stressors, but it has not worked on me yet![131] I did have one encounter a couple of years ago when a sand shark swam in front of my daughter and me. I never entered the ocean again during that vacation, even after our daughter, who was about five years old, said, *"Mom, come on, that big fish is gone now!"* I have been swimming in the ocean since that time, and as I watched my daughter dive through the ocean waves with my husband and her granddad, I was reminded of what it is like to be a kid and have no worries.

My prayer is that she will never have any fears or worries, but I know as a Christian she will unfortunately face similar stresses and fears that we all face as the devil is encircling us. It is important to find solutions to decrease stress and fears that we face on a daily basis, and it is our job as her parents to ensure she is prepared when those temptations, struggles, or stressors occur. I know one day my daughter will most likely imitate my similar Type A traits, and it is important to teach her to exhibit self-control in various life experiences. We need not forget that everyone around us is watching our reactions—both positive and negative. If we allow stress to ruin our lives, we may be faced with irreversible damage to our physical bodies, which could inhibit our ability to witness.

PREVENTING STRESS IN CHILDREN

Now that we understand the importance in coping, we can focus on preventative measures for those little people who are constantly watching us in the good times and the bad—our children. There are a couple of topics I would like to discuss in regards to preventing stress in children with Type A tendencies—who we all know will most likely turn into Type A adults.

Obviously, if children are raised by Type A parents, then they are definitely going to imitate several of our characteristics at some point. We are all familiar with the birth order theory, which suggests our personalities are affected by the order in which we are born. However, the influence on children's personalities may not truly be based on their actual birth order but perhaps in the parenting those children receive. One author writes that first-time parents provide *"undivided love and attention"* and set *"high expectations"* for their firstborn child; consequently, the firstborn child associates *"love with success"* and feels compelled to be a *"perfectionist"* in order to please his or her parents.[132]

All of these factors play a huge role in setting up the firstborn to inherit Type A characteristic traits. It is imperative to avoid placing our children on a pedestal for who we want them to be rather than watching them transform into the person God wants them to be. While the time we have to raise our children is so very limited, especially for working families, it is vital that we give our children just that... TIME. Time to grow and learn, time to teach and read, time to laugh and cuddle, time to ask questions and also answer questions, time to play and time to pray, and always time to love.

That's it, pure and simple! This works for your first child, second child, or how ever many children you are blessed to raise.

I have based this section of the book on a couple of blogs that I enjoyed reading, as the authors touched on very sensitive issues with how we are raising our children. As Type A parents, while we sometimes overcommit our schedules, we don't necessarily have to carry the same way of thinking into our children's schedules. Fortunately for us, God offers help to improve our behaviors and schedules, and He is more than ready to help us teach our children the same—we just need to pray and ask for daily guidance. God will bless us if we continue to put Him first in all that we do, and I hope reading this section will give you some insight on how to get started.

First, we are teaching our kids to rush through their days and multitask at a much earlier age. I don't know how many times my daughter has told me, *"Mom, I can't do three things at once!"* And she is absolutely right. Now, don't get me wrong, multitasking is sometimes a necessity, but if it is negatively affecting our children's performance and stress levels, then we should take a step back and evaluate where we need to improve. We should not be teaching our children to be in a rush all the time. Our children deserve more than our persistence in trying to make them mini-versions of our Type A selves.

I recently read a blog in which the title quickly grabbed my attention—*"The Day I Stopped Saying 'Hurry Up'"*—by Rachel Macy Stafford. Unfortunately, having a Type A personality and trying to meet my personal goals often involves my family in some way. I often find myself guilt-stricken because I am not spending quality time with my daughter because of my own desires and the schedule we maintain with work, school, church, sporting events, etc. Stafford and I share one thing in common—we both wish for extra time in the day to complete all of our tasks, but I found it amusing when she described her daughter *"as a gift"* to her Type A personality.[133]

Stafford, like most of us moms with *"overcommitted schedules,"* began many sentences to her daughter with *"hurry up"*—before eating, brushing her teeth, and even going to bed—while actually describing herself as a *"bully"* to her own children.[134] Yes, we are parents, and our children should be obedient to our requests, as long as we are obedient to God and follow principles within the Bible. However, we should never bully our children into functioning at adult speed. Truly, for those of us who are constantly saying, *"Hurry up,"* we should ask ourselves why we are always pressuring our children to be in a hurry?

For me, I know that I could get up earlier to start my day—instead of rushing to get myself and my daughter ready. I could also give myself extra time when my daughter and I are planning an outing. Designating extra time would prevent me from becoming angry and frantic when she needs to use the bathroom just before leaving, instead of twenty minutes before when I previously asked her. Stafford actually mentions in her blog that she apologized to her children for always rushing. She wanted to be more patient like them.

Our children are constantly discovering and perceiving information from the moment they are born and utilizing all of their senses to learn about their surroundings. When we as their parents create a sense of urgency all of the time, we may actually be decreasing their capacity to grow. We all should learn from our children by observing God's wonders with all of our senses, because when we rush, we don't always appreciate the beauty God has shown to us. Stafford ends her blog by saying that *"[p]ausing to delight in the simple joys of everyday life is the only way to truly live,"* and I completely agree.[135]

While children need to learn a sense of urgency for some events, it is okay for parents to learn to slow down and enjoy the simple things. Sing your child's favorite song in the car or maybe point out the beautiful animals as you drive from one location to the next. We must never, ever, forget to initiate prayer for any reason when on our way somewhere, even if it's to thank God for His miracles and to help us not to rush through our days... because as we get older, we realize that the days become shorter and shorter. I know one day I'll be waving goodbye to my daughter as she drives a car for the first time or giving her a hug and kiss as she goes to college. While our job as parents is to ensure our children are rooted in Christ, it is also our role to prepare them for the world they will face as adults. The stress they face will be tremendous, and if they do not know their Heavenly Father, they will have a difficult time navigating through a world whose morals are compromised on a daily basis.

We must allow our children to mature and grow rather than rushing them through. We need to spend time together as a family. It doesn't have to be an expensive outing. It is merely about spending time together. It is vital for our children to see they are more important than the items on our to-do lists. Always include devotion time with God as they learn how to improve their relationships with Him.

While we desire our children to avoid many of our worst behaviors, I do, however, believe there are several Type A traits children should learn, including a desire to work hard and complete goals. I persistently encourage my daughter to be creative and set high goals for where she might like to go to college or what she would like to name her future bakery, which is her current future profession. I want her to be independent and self-reliant; however, I also want her to submit to and follow the path God chooses for her. I thought I was doing a pretty good job of parenting during her younger years, but I never thought about the negative Type A traits she could acquire as she begins to model my behavior.

Every parent has had that *"uh-oh"* moment when your child mirrors your bad conduct, whether it is a poor choice of language or an undesirable action. For most parents, it only takes one time to notice a negative behavior in your child, and we immediately discourage similar future conduct or actions.

Nevertheless, we may be persistently repeating the same behavior our children are without realizing we are the source. If we as adults and parents continue in our adverse behavior, then how will our children ever learn Christ-like behavior? Or more importantly, how will they be set apart as believers if their actions are not Christ-like?

Once I realized Reese's negative behavior paralleled my own actions, I recognized many flaws and changes I needed to make myself. Consequently, my flaws are multiplied ten-fold when I see my daughter copying my same faults. I remember when she was about five years old and her responses to me started to change. While I recommended suggestions about her behavior, speech, and basic skills, she started responding with a very sarcastic *"FIIIIINNNNNE!"* Obviously, I quickly corrected her and we discussed the importance of showing respect. My husband gently pointed out that she most likely picked up this very negative response from me. I definitely did not believe him—until five minutes later, I said the same word in the exact same tone when I responded to my husband.

First, I hate when I am wrong... another Type A trait that my daughter and I unfortunately share, which is a work in progress. Second, I had just spoken to my daughter about showing respect when I disrespected my husband with my response. In the past, I have admitted to my husband and daughter when my behavior was not of the Spirit. In this particular instance, I humbly apologized to them both and talked with Reese about the reasons we needed to change.

Our behaviors are not always encouraging and definitely not uplifting for others. I want my daughter to understand that we are not perfect, and I want her to see that we try to improve ourselves based on biblical principles. This is why it is important to spend time with our children, so they can have Christian role models who show them the very essence of Christianity—love and grace. However, in order to spend quality time with our children, we need to prioritize our time and alter our demanding schedules.

Another online journal that intrigued my interest was a preacher's blog regarding over-commitment. Frank Powell states that parents are obsessed with keeping their children busy with activities. Today, our children suffer from over-commitment, and the only ones to blame are ourselves, the parents. Personally, I want my daughter to experience everything she can, as I know she will only be under our roof for a short time, and we always ask what sport she wants to play for the upcoming season, whether it's soccer, softball, gymnastics, volleyball, or basketball. My husband and I promote these activities as fun exercise, especially during the winter months in an attempt to deter her use of electronic devices.

Previously, we had only enrolled in one sport at a time and no other activities during my husband's busy baseball season. Recently, though, her activity level more than doubled. She is now taking piano lessons and participating in basketball, gymnastics, and learning a speaking part for her role in a local Christian theater play. After a couple of weeks of daily activities, she woke up on a Friday morning not feeling well and asked to miss school, which was an unusual request for Reese. I took her to my mother-in-law's house for the day, and after eight hours of no fever, tummyache, sore throat, or headache, I told my husband that she probably just needed a day off to rest—and I was right. She felt well enough to play in her basketball game the following morning.

I often worry that our days pass so quickly because of our busy schedules, and I have heard arguments on my friends' social media accounts for both sides where parents state they would prefer their children spend time in extracurricular activities as opposed to falling in with negative or even criminal behaviors—but when did we start allowing our schedules to become our obsession? And when did we let our over-committed schedules become more important than spending time as a family and with God? By maintaining this fast-paced life, we are encouraging fatigue in our children. As adults, we understand how a lack of rest affects our daily functions. It is multiplied by one hundred when our children do not rest—every parent knows that a sleepy child is a cranky child.

Unfortunately, a state of exhaustion may worsen stress within our children, just like with us. In recent studies, approximately 25-30% of our children do not get enough sleep.[136] The American Academy of Pediatrics (AAP) recommends school-age children sleep at least 9-12 hours per night and 8-10 hours for teenagers.[137] When sleep-deprived, our children may display significant mood changes, rebellious behavior, poor focus and concentration at school, and perhaps hyperactivity—including *"excessive talking"* and a lack of patience.[138]

≈

Our children are already facing an obesity crisis because of poor nutrition and lack of exercise, but missing out on sleep may also worsen symptoms of *"obesity, diabetes, and high blood pressure,"* as well as a weakened immune system leading to various illnesses.[139] The AAP also states a decrease in sleep may increase risk for injury during sports and may actually lead to a higher *"risk for self-harm or suicidal thoughts."*

Knowing this, why would anyone want to subject their kids to exhaustion by maintaining a busy schedule? I found one statement within this preacher's blog that really made me think. He said, *"Don't allow your family to worship the idol of over-commitment."*[140]

Powell further describes over-commitment as *"one of the great idols of American Christianity"* as it improves self-esteem and self-worth, but he also questions whose self-esteem is boosted, the child or the parent?[141] My husband, the coach, is not a fan of *"everyone's a winner"* and weekly championship rings and trophies, as these things only build a sense of pride within our children at an early age. Powell also states that we as parents *"enjoy the satisfaction"* but are merely *"sacrific[ing] our children on this altar"* of over-commitment.[142] In our last marriage retreat, we learned that instead of *"molding"* our children, we should *"unfold"* them. Children are a true blessing from the Lord. By allowing God to mold them into faithful Christian servants, we should encourage them to seek their own Christian walk as directed by God, and not force our own agenda out of selfish desires.

Powell believes that over-commitment may also lead to anxiety as these children grow into teenagers who are *"obsessed with outward achievements,"* much like that of Type A individuals.[143] It is important to allow our children to learn from small mistakes at a younger age, as this will train them to manage trials throughout their lives—no matter the size or stressor. On the other hand, if our children are frequently ridiculed, they may develop stress-induced anxiety as well as other undesirable body symptoms previously mentioned. They may dislike school because they have not learned how to cope with stress at an earlier age.

The Book of Ephesians reminds us that children are to obey their parents, and through their obedience, they are promised a longer life (6:1-3). However, we as parents, also have instructions not to provoke our children to anger with constant criticism because it evokes stress and diminishes respect. We are instructed to raise our children *"in the training and admonition of the Lord"* (Ephesians 6:4).

Today, our children face a very troubled world when out of our sight. They will encounter many temptations and may suffer consequences that we never dreamed about when we were younger—many thanks to social media. As parents, we must ask God for an understanding heart just as King Solomon did, and God will bless us and our families for putting Him first no matter the situation (I Kings 3-11-14). We also learn from the Book of Philemon when Paul writes that his heart was refreshed with *"joy and consolation"* by his fellow Christian supporters (1:7). Are we as parents refreshing the hearts of our children?

By our fruit, we should refresh the hearts of both Christians and non-believers, but also, more importantly, to those who learn directly from us. Our children should also find trust and confidence in us as both their parents and Christian mentors. We serve as our children's advocates in providing *"rest and renewal"* to their spirits when they are weakened by stress.[144]

I hope you are blessed to have a church with multiple Christian families to seek parenting guidance. Unfortunately, our community does not share the same family values. In recent years, our community has scheduled many sporting events that affect routine worship schedules on both Sunday mornings as well as Wednesday evenings. Our young children and youth are now expected to comply with schedules just as any adult going to work. And if they miss a game or practice, the consequence is to sit out a game, which can be detrimental to a child's self-esteem. This has also created chaos within our churches as we try to plan extracurricular activities not only around a family's work schedule, but also around our children's busy calendars. While I understand how important it is for our children to learn responsibility and discipline at a young age, I do recognize there are various ways to teach these principles to our youth and not just through multiple activities.

It's true that sometimes the work of a Christian will go unnoticed, and typically no trophies are given on earth for the work we do for Christ. Nonetheless, if our children are not attending church on a regular basis, then they will never learn of the eternal, heavenly rewards that God promises for our works. I understand fulfilling a child's dream of playing a sport or acting in a play, especially if they are talented and show potential, but we cannot *"sacrifice"* our children on these stages any longer. They should learn how to overcome adversity when they don't win a trophy every week or make the team. And it is equally important to teach them the benefits of serving others without receiving accolades, which is very different than what the world teaches them now.

Show your child you love them just for being your son or daughter—win or lose.

Teach them to overcome disappointment when they face trials.

Show them God's love and mercy—even when they fail.

We should always support our children's desires after they first learn to prioritize their commitments to God and then discover time management. By teaching our children at a young age to place the desires of others over their own, they will hopefully grow into respectful adults and disciples of God.

Do your children see you focusing your time and energy on doing works for Christ, and do you involve them? Don't you think God deserves our undivided attention and focus when we are working for Him? If we do not learn how to change our behaviors and patterns, then our children will never learn how to control their time appropriately. We should discuss our priorities for God, including a time to read the Bible, a time to pray, a time for church, and a time for mission work.

In conclusion, it is vital to teach our children not to put other people, events, or schedules above our relationships with God.

As parents, we should display godly behaviors for our children to mirror. We must teach them to be respectful of others, teach them not to discriminate against those with disabilities, teach them that God created us all differently, and teach them that just as we may not win a trophy or make a certain sports team, we are not going to win everyone to Christ. We must teach them to continue in their faith and teach them to keep going. As long as we continue to teach our children the importance of Christian-based principles, their destined roles as future Type A Christians will be used for good rather than evil.

STRESS CONCLUSIONS

Now that you have a better knowledge of various health risks associated with chronic stress, you can see how easily our bodies fatigue, both physically and psychologically. When God grants us time without obligations, it is essential to rest and set positive examples for our children. Again, stressors will vary from person to person, as well as its risk factors. While we now understand how to avoid likely stressors and consequences, we can start to recognize that unforeseen stressors are not meant to suppress our relationship with our Heavenly Father, but to enhance it. As we reach the final chapter, let's discuss the recommendations for utilizing the fruit of the Spirit, as well as obstacles we may face and how to overcome potential distractions. We'll also discuss the eternal rewards promised for those of us who bear fruit.

CHAPTER FIVE
TYPE A TRAITS VS. FRUIT OF THE SPIRIT

The initial theme for this book began after realizing Type A traits included both positive and negative features. As I shared before, I always thought having a Type A personality encompassed many great characteristics. I was always focused on school, my career, and any project that held my interest, which included studying for exams, planning a wedding, trying to become pregnant, and making our house a home. However, I started realizing that some of the traits I possessed did not necessarily pair with the attributes of the fruit of the Spirit.

This chapter will discuss the correlation between Type A traits and the individual nine attributes of fruit, as well as why they are recommended, how to identify our distractions, and how to prune ourselves for better growth. We will also talk about rewards that are promised from God. And you will see why I became so concerned with my own personality traits in comparison to the fruit we should develop as Christians.

THE FRUIT

Let's review the nine attributes produced by the Holy Spirit. As mentioned by Paul in the Book of Galatians, the fruit of the Spirit include *love, joy, peace, patience, kindness, goodness, faithfulness, meekness, and self-control* (5:22-23). Paul wrote this letter to the church of Galatia to indicate the followers of Jesus would be *"led by the Spirit and not by the law"* (Galatians 5:18). This was a time when the law served as a means to determine those who were actually faithful to God. However, after the resurrection of Jesus Christ, we have all been *"justified by faith"* (Romans 5:1) and *"the love of God has been poured out in our hearts by the Holy Spirit who was given to us"* (Romans 5:5). The fruit of the Spirit affects how we live, love, and behave on this earth toward God and our neighbors. These characteristics should be evident in all believers and should set us apart from those who choose to live in the flesh. We did not choose Jesus, rather He chose us to bear fruit in His name (John 15:16).

We simply cannot act as Christians on Sundays and lovers of the flesh on the other six days of the week. The Bible warns us that *"with the tongue we praise our Lord and Father, and with it we curse human beings, who have been made in God's likeness. Out of the same mouth comes praise and cursing"* (James 3:9-10). We can't go to work on Monday and instigate a conversation about a coworker after hearing the Word on

Sunday about gossiping. And, we shouldn't have the desire to post a *"funny"* yet rude social media post directed at someone else's expense.

Are we going to fail? I can answer for myself—Yes, I have failed many times. But we should prayerfully ask God to improve our faults through the Holy Spirit and grant us wisdom to overcome the flesh. We, as Christians, should strive to uphold these nine virtues each and every day. While our bodily forms were created in God's image (Genesis 1:27), our personalities should also be a reflection of God because He is a *"compassionate and gracious God [who is] slow to anger, abounding in love and faithfulness"* (Psalm 86:15).

We will first identify our weaknesses in our personalities, and after recognizing our own faults, we can then learn how to improve upon our usual tendencies. Now, while many individuals have various personality traits, hopefully we do not possess all of the negative traits. It is interesting, though, that for each attribute of the fruit of the Spirit, there is a negative Type A characteristic. Despite having the Holy Spirit living inside of us, we do not always listen to our Helper and instead allow the flesh to take over. We should always remember that *"the eyes of the Lord are in every place, keeping watch on the evil and the good"* (Proverbs 15:3). This suggests even in our darkest times that God is watching our behavior, along with many people around us.

OBSTACLES

We have many obstacles and distractions in our Christian walk that may cause internal conflict. This may be at home with our spouse or children, at work with coworkers, or even at church with fellow members. The devil is always at work and provokes both worry and anxiety in our lives, no matter the place or time. Satan is deviously working on our Christian marriages, causing destruction of Christian homes through adultery, selfish ambitions, poor financial management, and even extra-curricular activities, which includes sports, television, and other excessive commitments. Satan encourages our coworkers to be jealous and to gossip, which can lead to dissension in the workplace. The devil also works through the church to disrupt congregations, mostly by altering our impartial thoughts into biased perceptions of others and by increasing pride among believers. Satan knows God loves us so much that He sent his only Son to die on the cross to offer us the gift of salvation and eternal life (John 3:16). The devil would like nothing better than to cause turmoil in the lives of God's people. Therefore, we should always seek ways to edify one another to prevent the devil from desecrating our families, friends, and church congregations.

Perhaps another distraction is one deep within ourselves, which could be interpreted in two very distinct ways—our self-esteem and our pride. First, our self-esteem, or self-image, may be a distraction to utilizing our fruit of the Spirit if we are insecure or lack self-worth. Second, our fruit can be minimized if we are prideful due to an overabundance of confidence. My study Bible defines self-esteem as *"how each individual values herself [or himself].*"[145] Perhaps a common denominator is that Type A individuals are typically considered to be both loud extroverts and confident and sociable people. Some might even describe us as having higher self-esteems. This doesn't suggest we have to be overly confident in utilizing our fruit. Instead, we are to be humble as we allow His light to shine unto others. We are taught to be bold in our faith (Ephesians 3:11-12) as we maintain a positive sense of worth as a believer.

On the other hand, Type B personalities are usually considered introverts, or slightly more reserved or withdrawn, and could easily be mistaken for having a low self-esteem. Whether Type A or B, we as Christians should always value ourselves just as our Creator sees us. God doesn't care how many times we fall—He only cares about how many times we pick ourselves up again. Negative self-esteem may cause self-conviction, which prevents us from doing the work that God desires.[146] A *"healthy self-esteem"* as described in my study Bible includes (1) acceptance into Christ, (2) acknowledging the need for Jesus in our life, (3) understanding God's purpose for our lives, (4) fulfilling His will through good works, (5) avoiding comparisons to others, (6) appreciating the difference in working with others, and (7) remaining faithful in taking risks.[147]

Regardless of personality type, believers are to see the glass as half-full, not half-empty. If God blesses you with half of a glass, or even just one-fourth of a glass, we should continually praise the good Lord above for all His blessings upon us.

Everyone has a Christian family member, a teammate, a friend or coworker, or maybe even someone at church who is insecure and may be doubtful about his or her faith, but we as Christians have nothing to question. God loves so much that He sent His Son to die and cover all of our sins, even those sins that no one on earth knows about except God. We should never go through our Christian walk with feelings of inadequacy or skepticism. God deserves the glory no matter our situations, as we are taught to *"always rejoic[e]"* in times of tribulation (2 Corinthians 6:10). Even though we are created in God's image with different personalities, we have the utmost assurance in our future as we will be living with our Creator forever and ever.

How can any of us be half-empty with a promise like that?

There are many biblical characters within the Old and New Testament who did not portray a believer's self-esteem. Consider Ruth's mother-in-law, Naomi, who lost her husband and her two sons. She lost everything she thought was important and even gave herself the nickname, *"Mara,"* which meant God was bitter to her (Ruth 1:20). Fortunately, she developed a loving relationship with her daughter-in-law, Ruth, who, through her obedience, exalted God and restored Naomi's self-esteem.

How can we develop a positive Christian self-esteem? Well, *"we are [God's] workmanship, created in Christ Jesus for good works"* (Ephesians 2:10). James is a wonderful book in the Bible that discusses faith and works. He tells us that *"by works [our] faith [is] made perfect"* (James 2:22). Jesus presented two great commandments for Christians to fulfill when He stated we should *"love the Lord your God with all your heart, with all your soul, and with all your mind"* and *"love your neighbor as yourself"* (Matthew 22:37-39). I believe the first commandment requires faith and trust as we serve a God who is ultimately invisible to our physical eyes. This requires reading His Word and praying to Him on a daily basis in order to feel His presence. This also requires commitment and dedication in furthering our relationships with Him.

It is written, *"Blessed is the man who trusts in the Lord, and whose hope is the Lord"* (Jeremiah 17:7). For if we truly love God, then our attitudes should be ones of *love, joy, peace, patience, kindness, goodness, faithfulness, meekness, and self-control,* which are the fruit of the Spirit (Galatians 5:22). Being a loving and devoted follower of God should also promote a desire to do good works for our fellow neighbors. We are told in the Book of James that faith without works is dead (2:14) and *"that a man is justified by works, and not by faith only"* (2:24).

These are just a few ways to advance your Christian self-esteem or self-image. First, learn of God's love for you as you accept Him as your Creator. Second, study God's Word to prevent feelings of uncertainty or doubt as a Christian. And third, follow God's will in producing good fruit as you put others ahead of yourself. Our self-esteem is also enhanced when we understand the need for Christ in our lives and learn to love those who may be different from us. When we put others ahead of ourselves, we can avoid the distraction of low self-esteem, which will further cultivate our fruit.

A second internal factor that may be a distraction from living a Godly life is pride or being proud of a particular quality or skill. Now, for those of you who possess a natural-born talent, like singing, gymnastics, athletics, and even public speaking, you may have a difficult time acknowledging God since your skill developed at a younger age. For example, I remember studying for previous nursing tests and being jealous of an intelligent friend who didn't need to study as much as I did and maintained better grades than most of us. Was it wrong for her to display these abilities? Certainly not! She never bragged on herself; instead, she tried to edify the rest of us as she listened to our test-taking anxieties. I realize now she could have portrayed an arrogant behavior, and we probably would not have become such good friends if she had not been so humble with her gifts.

God blesses each of us with spiritual gifts and talents for us to use at particular moments in our lives; however, when we become prideful, our gifts or talents may be taken away, sometimes without us even realizing why. There are those who take pride in their profession, and others who may take pride in their family. For those who take pride in their career, they may devote all of their time for tasks related to their jobs and leave no time for God.

You may be wondering, how do we tackle pride in our family? Well, we may focus all our efforts in caring for our family physically and emotionally when these actions will never satisfy our own spiritual needs, especially when we devote much of our time away from God. Furthermore, our focus spent on other priorities may never promote an environment for our family to grow spiritually. If we dedicate our time to running our young children to various events and not to church or Christian-related activities, is it worth it in the end to have a pretty good athlete over a maturing Christian child? One might argue that they can do both. Well, yes, they can, but we need to ensure our families are teaching humility in serving others first rather than winning championships for self-gain.

The Book of Philippians states, *"Let nothing be done through selfish ambition or conceit, but in lowliness [humility] of mind let each esteem others better than [yourselves]"* (2:3). It is essential to understand humility and truly thank God for all he has given us, including our special talents and gifts, that we might impact someone along our way. If one can learn humility and denial of self at a younger age, then an abundance of blessings will occur for all involved.

Learning to overcome pride may be very difficult, but I found a wonderful article written by the former Dr. Henry Brandt that describes how to do this in five easy steps:[148]

1. Adopt a Correct View of God
2. Revise Our False Beliefs
3. Repent of Our Sins
4. Defend Ourselves Against Spiritual Attacks
5. Flee Temptations

The first step is to adopt a correct view of God, which means in order to respect God, we must first learn that God is *"superior"* and has *"supreme authority"* over us. Dr. Brandt advises that to complete this first step, we must *"ask God to reveal Himself more clearly to [us]."*

The second step is to revise our false beliefs. Dr. Brandt states we must stop viewing ourselves as superior to others. He also says that *"pride is the single greatest obstacle to loving people,"* and we should become someone full of *"self-denial and grace-filled humility."*

The third step in overcoming pride is to repent of our sins. This sounds like the easiest of the first few steps, right? If you said no, then you are definitely correct. It is very difficult for me to admit when I am wrong, probably more than anyone in my family. I hate that feeling more than anything, but in order to be more Christ-like, we must pray to God specifically for forgiveness and not just mention it as a blanket statement. We read throughout the Bible of God's forgiveness—all we have to do is ask. I have told my daughter many times that we are essentially writing our sins on a chalkboard (i.e. dry erase board because she has no idea what a chalkboard is). Then God erases each one as we ask forgiveness; we need to realize that Christ died for all of our sins—past, present, and future. When we ask God to pardon us, we should also give thanks to Jesus for taking the punishment for each sin we have committed.

Step four discussed by Dr. Brandt is to defend ourselves against spiritual attacks. He suggests that we can actually *"become proud of [our] humility."* How can that happen? He describes this as our flesh overcoming the spirit. When we are placed on a pedestal at home, at work, or maybe even at church, we may become prideful. The attention is not always desired, but it definitely feels rewarding when we receive it. Dr. Brandt states we should *"seek to magnify God, not God's creatures"* and realize *"that God is the one who deserves honor, not [us]."*

The fifth and final step in overcoming pride as an obstacle in fulfilling God's will in our lives is to flee temptation. Dr. Brandt warns of endless temptations we will encounter as we face a mighty evil power. We can, just as Jesus did, call on God and rely on the Holy Spirit to aid in resistance. Dr. Brandt gives us four methods to decrease temptations by *"focusing on [our] relationships with God, [claiming] God's promises, establish[ing] safeguards, and expect[ing] victory."* Everyone will face persecution at some point in life. However, the devil creates temptations when our faith is weak which often leads to poor choices. When we are *not* spiritually mature in God's Word, we may become more tolerant and perhaps engage in sinful behavior that is discouraged in the Bible. When we are spiritually mature and fully submit to our Creator, we are better equipped to flee temptations as we rely on the victorious power of the Holy Spirit.

To review, in order to overcome pride, first, we must pray and seek a relationship with God.[149] Second, we must be knowledgeable of Scripture and be ready *"in season and out of season"* (2 Timothy 4:2). Third, just as we make changes to our diet and exercise routine, we must make *"lifestyle"* changes. Next, what Brandt recommends is truly remarkable. He tells us to ask a friend to hold us accountable, volunteer in a place we would typically never visit, throw away all our make-up if we are proud of our looks, or perhaps even trade in our fancy car.[150] Wow, the nerve of him to tell us that? Unfortunately, I know exactly what he is trying to suggest, and I pray that you will too. These are pretty demanding recommendations, but he delivers his point without room for discussion.

We all have our vices, or dare I say idols, and in order to put God first, maybe this is the best way to learn true humility. Does God care that we drive a fancy car or buy the most expensive make-up? No, of course not! So when is it time to remove the material things that take up room in our hearts, that is different for each of us, and we have to listen to the Holy Spirit to ensure our prideful lusts do not interfere with our ability to grow our fruit.

A quote by Florence Littauer says, *"The purpose of pruning is to improve the quality of the roses, not to hurt the bush."*[151] This is true, as sometimes we have to *"trim the fat"* as we say in the South, which means that in order to grow better fruit, we must trim away what is holding us down. If a fancy boat or car payment is preventing you from tithing, then you may need to think about where your priorities lie. If you spend more time promoting yourself than Jesus, then it's time to reevaluate your spiritual maturity. Most likely, each of us is trying to enjoy all that God has to offer on this earth, myself included, but when we start sacrificing our time and money and talents for idols, then it's time to deep clean.

Lastly, Brandt doesn't want us to just hope for victory in overcoming our prideful ways but to demand or expect it to happen. He tells us not to focus on the past, but look forward to the future in anticipation for all the wonderful things that we might accomplish by giving God the glory for it all.[152]

I will admit that in writing this book I have been surprised by how everything has come together, including the discovery of this wonderful outline regarding pride. That said, I must remember that even though God has blessed me with the talent to bring this book together, it is for *His* glory and not mine.

PRUNING FOR GROWTH

Now that we have discussed some ways that hinder us from developing our fruit, let's take a look at some ways that promote growth.

First and foremost, we need to be true followers of the Word. God tells us that we are blessed if we are faithful and put our trust in Him rather than men (Jeremiah 17:5-10). In today's society with endless social media outlets, we, adults and children alike are influenced by so many who are not Christians as well as those who claim to be positive role models but whose roots are not in Christ. We must make conscious efforts to change our thought patterns and actions to those of Christ. I have struggled many times with whether to cancel my own social media accounts, but I have not yet. I currently serve as the primary operator for our church's social media, posting various events and encouraging Scripture verses or Christian music videos. When scrolling through social media, I have often been uplifted by posts from countless individuals and church affiliates, which is the tone I try to maintain on my own accounts.

On the other hand, I have sometimes also walked away with a different attitude than when I started, usually one of discouragement. My husband's name was recently slandered on social media based on his role as the high school head baseball coach. Since my husband is someone I love and respect with all my heart, I became very angry and wanted to respond in writing. I'm sure negative comments had been verbalized before about my husband, but I wasn't aware and therefore remained unaffected. This time, however, when I actually read what was posted, I rehearsed a proper retort in my head several times. And trust me, I had some very negative things to say. However, I realized that I should follow in my husband's footsteps and just be quiet—which is what Jesus taught us to do as His own name was slandered prior to His crucifixion.

I was very upset but quickly understood that God was preparing me. If I could not withstand persecution on a small scale, then I would never be able to face it on a much larger scale. And, as my husband completes seminary school and this book is published, I realize that many more opportunities for persecution may arise, and we will face many questions, perhaps even intimidation, from those who oppose Christianity. Luckily, my husband laughed off the incident, and after several days, the negative thoughts in my mind seemed to gradually disappear.

I know my husband is a wonderful coach who displays his Christian morals for all to see—something many schools are not fortunate to have. I also realized the need to pray for Rob's critic. After much prayer, I made a conscious decision not to post a reply in my husband's defense. By not posting, I was listening to the Holy Spirit and my God-fearing husband who is the leader of our Christian home. He consistently receives many texts and accolades from former players, and they are not only thankful for his teachings on baseball, but also life in general. I know he humbly appreciates those texts, and the many acts of gratitude definitely outweigh the few malicious posts.

Learning to face such attacks may be daily for some or rare for others. I don't know which would be easier—one might grow accustomed to such assaults and learn to ignore them where another might face never-ending stress and anxiety. We must continue to face the world with Christian behavior no matter how the world treats us. This is the only way to grow and overcome when tribulation occurs.

Speaking of my husband, he recently gave a sermon discussing fruitful growth for our lives. He spoke of the sequence in finding and discovering spiritual gifts, which is perfect for learning how to grow our own fruit of the Spirit. The apostle Peter tells us to be persistent, *"giving all diligence, add[ing] to your faith virtue, to virtue knowledge, to knowledge self-control, to self-control perseverance, to perseverance godliness, to godliness brotherly kindness, and to brotherly kindness love. For if these things are yours and abound, you will neither be barren nor unfruitful in the knowledge of our Lord Jesus Christ"* (2 Peter 1:5-8).

First, just as the verse describes, we must ask for wisdom just as Solomon did in order to better educate ourselves and to be transformed from the inside out. Then, we must realize these gifts build upon each other as God provides certain life experiences, including trials and tribulations. In order to better utilize our gifts, we must gain confidence and discipline in the place of adversity, which is the very definition of perseverance. When we *"never grow tired of doing good"* as mentioned in Galatians (6:9), we can then improve our characteristics of godliness only with the strength of God. Although I was hurt by disrespectful comments on social media regarding my husband, we are commanded to forgive our offenders. When questions arise and thoughts of retaliation enter our minds, we must rely on God's Word in showing agape love, even when it is not returned.

Peter describes the value in bearing fruit, which helps us to be effective and productive in our knowledge of Jesus Christ. He also warns that without these gifts, we are blind to Jesus' purpose on earth, which was to be the perfect Lamb of God who died for all of our sins and was resurrected to welcome us to our eternal home in Heaven. For when we admit our sins and believe in Jesus Christ as our Savior, we are promised access to Heaven and will be acknowledged for all the fruit we humbly displayed on Christ's behalf.

Peter described our admittance into Heaven similar to the welcome entrance for an Olympic champion.[153] I found this interesting as my hometown of Kingsport has an eight-kilometer (five-mile) race called the *"Crazy 8's."* It has also gained the title of the *"World's Fastest 8K,"* in which runners from all over the world come to compete. It is amazing to watch international-al runners, specifically Kenyan athletes, run with such vigor. It is even better to cheer those from our home town as they try to claim the title. The race is held during our annual summer festival titled *"Fun Fest"* where runners compete during the infamous night race. The finish line ends on the football field where the largest high school band in Tennessee marches on Friday nights in the fall.

Now, I have only run one 5K race (~3 miles), and I felt great after completing that race. The epitome of any race for me, though, would be to run into that stadium with fans cheering on both sides welcoming families and friends as loud music fills the stadium. There is also an overhead video board depicting the smiles of all the accomplished participants as they cross the finish line. It gives me chills just thinking about it! My husband has run it several times, and our daughter has been the excited recipient of his participation medals for the past several years. I can only imagine a greater welcome to runners who complete the infamous Boston Marathon—but still, this is *no* comparison to the welcome we will receive as we enter the gates of Heaven!

Peter tells us that our entrance to Heaven will be one of abundance or lavishness, but our only requirement is to be diligent in God's Word, steadfast in our faith, and humble for the remission of our sins (2 Peter 1:9-11). Can you imagine being welcomed into the gates of Heaven with not just unfamiliar spectators cheering for you, but family and friends who have passed on before? You may run through the gates hugging your parents, grandparents, siblings, cousins, and best friends. You might even give high-fives to Matthew, Mark, Luke, or John. What a day it will be!

Peter also tells us, just as he and other Christians who have passed on before, that we are to follow in their example and to fulfill the Great Commission as Jesus commanded (Matthew 28:19-20). The Holy Spirit gives us power to obtain and embrace all of these virtuous attributes as we remember Peter's encouragement for us to *"grow in the grace and knowledge of our Lord and Savior Jesus Christ"* (2 Peter 3:18) and *"in all things God may be glorified through Jesus Christ"* (1 Peter 4:11). Paul also describes his Christian walk as he *"fought the good fight... finished the race... [and] kept the faith"* (I Timothy 4:7).

My preacher once spoke during a sermon, saying Paul doesn't say that he actually won the fight, but he *finished* the race. Paul had many life experiences in which he probably felt like he failed. For example, he probably had times when others would not listen to his testimony or were too afraid of him, but Paul knew that once his sight was restored, he needed to carry out God's will in bringing others to know and follow Christ.

Paul also says in the first Book of Corinthians that he became a servant to all men, both Jews and Gentiles, submitting to their customs in order to bring them to Christ (10:19-23). We can't expect to only go to church and witness to other Christians who already have salvation. Don't get me wrong, not everyone in the church is saved, and many will benefit from your testimony in coming to salvation as well as gain wisdom from your trials and tribulation. However, that is not what we have been called to do.

Jesus tells us to go out, which means, we should go out... out of our comfort zones to reach others.

This might be to a homeless shelter or soup kitchen, a hospital or nursing home, a children's club or school, or even your work. For some, it might be a call to go into the mission field around the world, reaching those who have yet to hear God's Word. It is a little easier when trying to use your spiritual gifts around people you know in the church yet a little different when you are around non-believers or those who have never received the Word. Your previous confidence in your faith may wither at the thought of going out of your comfort zone, but when we realize who is in our corner, then who could ever be against us (Romans 8:31)?

For example, my sister-in-law and I have volunteered for the last several years at church during our annual vacation Bible school (VBS). We pretty much make fools of ourselves in front of everyone in our church, both adults and children, as we perform skits, sing, dance, and attempt suggested experiments. Every year the VBS director asks for our participation, and while it is a lot of preparation, especially for both of us who work full-time jobs, I am reminded of our pastor who always says that *"if you're going to make a fool of yourself, then be a fool for Jesus"* (I Corinthians 4:10). My sister-in-law and I pretty much fit that bill as we entertain all the youth and church members during those four summer days. Obviously, the ultimate goal is to share the Gospel and lead others, specifically our youth, to Jesus.

Is performing for our church audience out of our comfort zones? Well, we both love to sing and listen to music, but if we were performing in front of our professional colleagues, I'm pretty sure we would be a little more embarrassed and uncomfortable.

It is important to witness to both Jew and Gentile, both friends and enemies, and even coworkers and strangers. My sister-in-law and I both want to *"press toward the goal for [our] prize of the upward call of God in Christ Jesus"* in order to do God's will (Philippians 3:14). Our lives on earth are very short and temporary, but by continuing to run the race, we will all receive our eternal crowns. That's exactly what I plan to do, but for any Type A individual, it must be on the to-do list.

God prepares us for each phase of life and provides us with so many opportunities. We must ensure that our seemingly never-ending daily schedules also detail our responsibilities for Christ, not just ballgames and menus. Wouldn't it be great if our calendar included our plans for Christ along with our hair appointments and work deadlines? For those of us with crazy day-to-day schedules, we must make conscious efforts to be willing servants of Christ, and only then will God honor our desire to serve and provide us with opportunities.

Another option to grow our fruitful spirits is to seek and surround ourselves with those who are both admirable leaders and obedient to the Word of God. In the Book of Ezekiel, he uses a metaphor of a vine's strong branches (Israel) that withered away (disobedience and poor leadership) and became fruitless (lack of obedience to God) (19:10-14). It is essential to have great leaders in the church and in the home. Without God-fearing leaders in our lives, we would crumble just like those in the Old Testament who chose idols over their Creator (Ezekiel 20:8). I can surely attest to God who answered my prayers and probably the prayers of my parents when He blessed me with a godly husband. I am truly thankful for him and for his recent acceptance of his own calling as a minister.

I wonder, even now, where would I be in my Christian walk without him? Would I be this involved in church, or would I even be going at all if I married someone else? I hope that I would still be practicing my fruit as a believer, but if I did not have strong leadership within our current marriage and family, I can't truly say where I would be. I know my life has been full of choices, and I thank God above for revealing the paths I needed to take as well as the ones I needed to avoid. I think some of my experiences in previous relationships have allowed me to be more appreciative of my husband.

Unfortunately, due to my controlling Type A personality, I sometimes try to overshadow my husband in an attempt to take over the reigns as leader in our home. This is mostly due to my position as a health care provider where I make daily decisions for not only the health of my patients, but also our unborn patients who are equally as important. These are decisions that I do not take lightly. Sometimes, without realizing it (okay, maybe I do realize it and still do it), I assume the role of leader in my own home as I have trouble in fulfilling my role as his helper—not because I think he is incapable of making difficult decisions when it comes to our home and family, but because I think my ideas and opinions are perhaps better than his. (Wow! That felt good to get off of my chest.)

I feel that it is very challenging for women in Christ to hold positions of power or authority in our careers and then come home to a submissive role to our spouse and children. It is essential to realize our *"careers provide only part of a woman's identity. Ultimately, a woman is not what she does but who she is, which is largely determined by her relationship with God and [with] others."*[154] I am, however, blessed to have a husband who is understanding of my strengths, and I am learning to acknowledge him as the good leader that I know he is. By allowing him to lead, I am surrendering to God's plan for our Christian family. When I put myself ahead of my husband, I deprive my family from receiving many blessings. I know my fruit has increased solely because of my husband's obedience to God, and he continually encourages me to become a better Christian.

My hope is that I will never cease from yielding fruit because of my prideful personality. I know I am not perfect, and *"we all have sinned and fall[en] short of the glory of God"* (Romans 3:23). We have an ever-growing need to show non-believers that we are not hypocrites living perfect lives, but instead we are just sinners trying to live holy lives. Unfortunately, the people of this day and time are compelled to live a life of perfection. Now that we are all connected by social media, there is a total lack of privacy for which we have only ourselves to blame. We feel the need to stage our lives into the appearance of having the perfect marriage, perfect kids, perfect body, perfect job, perfect home, perfect pet, perfect birthday parties, and now even the perfect church activities.

Various home design shows on television have shown the importance of staging in selling homes. Staging is preparing a house for buyers to see it in its most beautiful and perfected state, with furniture and accessories that hide possible flaws that may exist. After purchasing a house, I would imagine the disappointment of arriving to an empty home that was previously staged. The cracks in the walls are now visible where pictures once hung, the floors creak in areas where rugs were once located, and old appliances no longer match previous finishes. It is funny how we as individuals feel the need to *"stage"* our own lives in order to portray ourselves as perfect in the world's eyes—all the while hiding under the imperfections that should bring us closer to God. A humble spirit is a necessity when asking forgiveness from God without trying to hide behind our faults.

I admit to wanting to have all aspects of my life organized, but when I went to nurse practitioner school, I knew I was going to have to let some things go in order to focus on obtaining my degree. I was nursing my daughter at the time with very little energy, and I was completely overwhelmed by all of my assignments. The house might have been a little messier, but in reality, the best thing for me was learning to let go of the irrelevant. We must realize that *"we"* are what's important—not having a perfectly clean house, not having our spouse's shirts ironed, not packing the perfect school lunch, and not having the best hair and make-up. It's the interactions that we have with one another that are important. Staging our lives may allow others to see only the positives, but it can depreciate our Christian walk and may also deter our ability to witness to non-believers. We must be honest in our testimonies as we share our ongoing trials and how God continues to deliver us from our imperfect ways.

Perhaps the best quote I have read on this matter is from my study Bible which says, *"The foremost trait you are called to perfect in your life is the ability to love."*[155] I am the first to admit that I would like every day to run smoothly without any hiccups. However, we all know that's not how the world works. I try to give 100% whether at home or work or church, but I know that I am going to fail at times. Not every patient will approve of my recommendations, my daughter will most assuredly disagree with rules when she becomes a teenager, and I know the church praise team may not want to sing all the songs I want to sing.

The Bible tells us that we are not perfect except *"God's love that has been perfected in us"* (I John 4:12). God's love is perfect, and we are to show others that example of perfect, sacrificial love. And, as Peter tells us, without love, we are nothing (I Corinthians 13:2). If we truly love people in the same regard as we love our spiritless priorities and possessions of this world, our marriages, families, and congregations will most definitely prevail.

We will undoubtedly face persecution because not everyone will choose to listen to us or even agree with our thoughts or beliefs. We are told in the last days to *"turn away"* from individuals who are *"lovers of themselves, lovers of money, boasters, proud, blasphemers, disobedient to parents, unthankful, unholy, unloving, unforgiving, gossipers, no self-control, brutal, despisers of good, traitors, headstrong, haughty, lovers of pleasure rather than lovers of God"* (2 Timothy 3:2-4). However, we are to remain faithful and *"thoroughly equipped for every good work"* as we continue doing God's will that others might see Him in us (2 Timothy 3:17).

The Book of Ephesians identifies the purpose for having spiritual gifts, which is the *"edifying of the body of Christ, till we all come to the unity of the faith and of the knowledge of the Son of God, to a perfect man, to the measure of the stature of the fullness of Christ"* (4:12-13). Our personalities are a direct reflection of the spiritual gifts granted by God. I imagine these gifts are based upon our personalities and how we are best suited to accomplish God's work on earth. The *"diversities of gifts"* include wisdom, knowledge, faith, healing, performing of miracles, prophecy, discerning of spirits, and speaking and interpreting of tongues. *"All these are the work of one and the same Spirit, and He distributes them to each one, just as He determines"* (I Corinthians 12:4, 8-11). Our goal is to accomplish the work of God in sharing the Gospel until we either pass to Heaven or we are caught up to Him.

I once heard a sermon on my morning commute discussing the joy of reaching the age of retirement as a Christian. I never thought about this until I heard this sermon on the radio. As a Type A individual, I obviously have plans for when my husband and I retire. First, I dream of being able to sit on our deck while drinking a cup of coffee in an actual coffee mug—not in a travel tumbler with a torn seal that leaks every time I try to take a sip, but in an actual oversized mug, so I can add as much creamer as I want. Second, my husband and I dream of traveling. He wants to see Italy, and I want to visit Hawaii. Both of these venues are full of exciting new things to experience, like the delicious cuisine in Italy and the breathtaking views in Hawaii. My husband also has dreams of purchasing a recreational vehicle to travel to all the SEC (Southeastern Conference) ballgames and watch every sport played. I would also like to grow a vegetable and herb garden. And, of course, spend time with our grown daughter and any grandchildren we are blessed to treasure.

Now, all of these plans are wonderful, but I never truly thought about what kind of plans I would do for the Lord when I retire as a nurse practitioner. Never! I never thought about what I could do for the One who has provided me all of my blessings on earth as well as the eternal blessings I have yet to see. We should never consider retiring from doing God's work. In fact, we should have more time to do His will after we retire from our earthly jobs. I look up to so many in my church who travel to other countries to build churches or provide health care to those in need, while others help with our local food pantries and travel to prisons to minister as Christian witnesses. Although I do provide a service to the women in our community, I admit to being a little jealous as I don't have the time for all of the things I would like to do to serve others.

My husband and I never really thought about these things until he received his calling. We started talking about what it would mean for him if he became a preacher and what it would mean for me as well. It does, however, bring a smile to my heart to think about all the things I could accomplish in the years to come. I had never thought of what I could do for the church, events I could assist with in the community, or perhaps even women's shelters I could offer my assistance to as both a nurse and a Christian.

While we now understand that retirement is just a phase of time, we should all look forward to our future on Earth and ask for God's blessings for our health and the ability to further His Kingdom when we finally reach retirement. We should also ask God to guide us in ways we can serve Him when we finally reach this time in our lives. God will grant us opportunities if we ask him. Remember, *"He who sows sparingly will also reap sparingly, and he who sows bountifully will also reap bountifully"* (2 Corinthians 9:6). God may have other ideas for my husband and me in the future, but I am excited to see where He will use us and how we can fulfill His will.

REWARDS

What does having a Type A personality have to do with the fruit of the Spirit? Well, pretty much everything. Our personality is what makes us distinct from others and puts emphasis on our spiritual gifts we have been granted. Peter tells us in the New

Testament that Christians—not just Israelites, but all followers of Christ—are God's *"chosen generation,"* and we are to be *"a peculiar people"* (1 Peter 2:9). There are various synonyms for the word *"peculiar,"* which include the following: odd, strange, weird, unusual, uncharacteristic, unconventional, unique, distinctive, and particular. Now all of these words are very similar, but a little different just like us. Dr. Hayden defines the word peculiar *"from the Latin word, 'pecus' which means 'flock'. The [King James Version] KJV translators were simply reflecting the idea that believers in Christ are the unique possession of God—they are His flock."*[156] We all have various personalities, and we are to use our personalities as God intended to further His Kingdom.

Therefore, if someone cuts in line while you are waiting to get movie tickets, are you going to get mad, huff and puff, or verbally accuse them of cheating? If someone sees you praying at your work lunch room and rolls their eyes at you, will you continue to pray or will you stop? What if someone steals something from your child at school? What if it is your child's most prized possession? What will your conversation be like with your child? Will it be one of anger and disgust, or will you discuss with your child that the perpetrator may not be as fortunate as your child? The accused may have never had anything to call his or her own. He or she may also have ungodly parents and have never been shown true love. Just as Peter told Christians in the New Testament that if we show uncharacteristically good traits and uphold our Christian morals for others, that *"they may, by your good works...glorify God"* (1

Peter 2:12) and *"put to silence the ignorance of foolish men"* (2 Peter 2:15).

In conclusion, Christians have various roles to fulfill in our daily Christian walk. In my years of working in health care, there are many different positions that function as a whole—all of which are deemed necessary to fulfill a service to a patient. Similarly, Christians also serve in different roles by the spiritual gifts they possess. Some are great ministers and some are better singers, while others are more suited as leaders, teachers, and planners. While we seek to understand our roles in serving as witnesses for Christ, it is essential to understand that our personalities should enhance, not diminish, our fruit of the Spirit as we fulfill our good works.

As Christians, we are running the race for *"imperishable crown[s]"* in Heaven and not for display on Earth (1 Corinthians 9:24-25). We should not let anyone, not even the devil, stand in our way of being overcomers for Christ.

In the Gospel of Matthew, Jesus spoke the lesson of the fig tree which grew leaves but no fruit (21:18-22). We are to be fruitful in our works just as the faithful church in the Book of Revelations who perseveres in keeping God's Word, never denying His name before others (3:7-13). Christians should not display a deceiving appearance when bearing fruit, but one of a faithful follower in keeping the Lord's commandments by loving one another and spreading the Gospel to non-believers. It is our role to surprise others through our actions by showing grace rather than judgment for those who do not know our Father. Just as the Book of Matthew tells us, the *"Son of Man will come in the glory of His Father with His angels, and then He will reward each according to his works"* (16:27). I, for one, find comfort and excitement in this verse—even as a professed Type A Christian.

My prayer in closing this book is for other Christians to display an overabundance of fruit toward others and to realize that selfless behavior is glorifying unto our Heavenly Father. And just like that, our commandments given by Jesus are fulfilled. If you have a Type A personality, I pray you have a better understanding of how to use your personality for God's will and hopefully have determined which traits to prune and which traits to grow. For those of you who are not Type A, I pray you continue to show patience to other Type A Christians so your relationships will be refreshed as you appreciate each other's strengths and weaknesses. As mentioned in the Book of Romans, we are one in the body of Christ but have different roles and functions in sharing the Gospel.

Thank you God for giving us the courage to be bold in our faith and granting us unique personalities in order to share Your love with others.

~Amen

NOTES

1. Unless otherwise noted, all biblical passages referenced are in the New King James Version (Nashville: Thomas Nelson Publishers, 1995).
2. Quotations book, accessed on September 23, 2017 from http://quotationsbook.com/quote/5983/
3. http://www.dictionary.com/browse/personality
4. Katerina Michouli, *"The Four Temperament Types of Hippocrates,"* accessed October 2, 2017 from https://katerinamichouli.wordpress.com/the-four-temperament-types-of-hippocrates-wikipedia/
5. S. A. McLeod, *"Wilhelm Wundt,"* 2008, accessed October 2, 2017 from www.simplypsychology.org/wundt.html
6. *"Behind Personality Tests,"* 2017, accessed October 1, 2017 from https://www.online-psychology-degree.com/personality-tests/
7. S. A. McLeod, *"Carl Jung,"* 2014, accessed October 2, 2017 from www.simplypsychology.org/carl-jung.html
8. A. McLeod *"Sigmund Freud."* 2013. Accessed October 2, 2017 from www.simplypsychology.org/Sigmund-Freud.html
9. McLeod, *"Carl Jung,"* 2014.
10. S.A. McLeod, *"Erik Erikson,"* last modified 2017, accessed October 16, 2017 from https://www.simplypsychology.org/Erik-Erikson.html
11. Ibid.
12. Ibid.
13. Ibid.
14. Ibid.
15. McLeod, *"Sigmund Freud,"* 2013.
16. *"Behind Personality Tests,"* 2017.
17. *"Type in Personal Growth,"* 2017, accessed October 2, 2017 from http://www.myersbriggs.org/type-use-for-everyday-life/type-in-personal-growth/
18. *"The Story of Isabel Briggs,"* accessed October 2, 2017 from https://www.capt.org/mbti-assessment/isabel-myers.htm?bhcp=1
19. Kendra Cherry, *"What is Personality and Why Does It Matter?"* last modified July 20, 2017, accessed October 16, 2017 from https://www.verywell.com/what-is-personality-2795416

20. Ibid.

21. Saul McLeod, *"Type A Personality,"* last modified 2014, accessed March 10, 2017 from http://www.simplypsychology.org/personality-a.html

22. Alex Mayyasi, *"The Invention of The Type A Personality,"* February 16, 2016, accessed October 2, 2017 from https://priceonomics.com/the-invention-of-the-type-a-personality/

23. Ibid.

24. McLeod, *"Type A Personality,"* 2014.

25. Mayyasi, *"The Invention,"* 2016.

26. McLeod, *"Type A Personality,"* 2014.

27. Joseph Chris, *"Personality Types A B C D Explained,"* February 18, 2016, accessed October 17, 2017 from http://www.josephchris.com/personality-types-a-b-c-d-explained

28. M. Farouk Radwan, *"A b c d personality types,"* last modified 2017, accessed October 17, 2017 from https://www.2knowmyself.com/a_b_c_d_personality_type

29. Ibid.

30. Chris, *"Personality Types,"* 2016.

31. Ronald E. Riggio, *"Are you Type A B or D Personality?"* August 23, 2014, accessed from https://www.psychologytoday.com/blog/cutting-edge-leadership/201408/are-you-type-b-or-d-personality

32. McLeod, *"Type A Personality,"* 2014.

33. Sirri, L., G. A. Fava, J. Guidi, P. Porcelli, C. Rafanelli, A. Bellomo, S. Grandi, L. Grassi, P. Pasquini, A. Picardi, R. Quartesan, M. Rigatelli, and N. Sonino, *"Type A Behaviour: A Reappraisal of Its Characteristics in Cardiovascular Disease." International Journal of Clinical Practice* 66, no. 9 (September 2012): 854-861, accessed July 1, 2017, from http://www.medscape.com/viewarticle/769623

34. Ibid.

35. Ibid.

36. Ibid.

37. Ibid.

38. Mayyasi, *"The Invention,"* 2016.

39. L. Sirri, et al., *"Type A Behaviour,"* September 2012.

40. Ibid.

41. *"Behind Personality Tests,"* 2017.

42. *"The Story of Isabel Briggs,"* 2017.

43. Palacio, R. J. *"Wonder."* February 14, 2012, accessed May 12, 2018, from https://www.goodreads.com/quotes/847679-we-carry-with-us-as-human-beings-not-just-the

44. Hellerman, Joseph. *"Our Priorities Are Off When Family Is More Important Than Church."* August 4, 2016, accessed May 12, 2018, from http://christianitytoday.com/ct/2016/august-web-only/if-our-families-are-more-important-than-our-churches-we-nee.html

45. Paul Hudson. *"The 25 Things That People With Type A Personalities Do."* February 11, 2014, accessed March 10, 2017 from http://elitedaily.com/life/motivation/the-25-things-that-people-with-type-a-personalities-do/

46. 88.3, WCQR, accessed March 18, 2018 from https://www.wcqr.org/wcqr-drive-thru-difference/

47. *Turning Point.* David Jeremiah, aired on WHCB: The Blessing, November 10, 2017.

48. Marla Cilley. *FlyLady.net.* Modifies daily, accessed from http://www.flylady.net

49. Ibid.

50. Elizabeth Scott, *"Type A Personality Traits; What Does It Mean to Have A Type A Personality?"* Last modified 2016, accessed March 10, 2017 from http://www.verywell.com/type-a-personality-traits-3145240

51. Ibid.

52. Hudson, *"25 Things,"* 2014.

53. Ibid.

54. Ibid.

55. Ronald E. Riggio, *"Are you a Type A or B Personality? Achievement Addicted or Laid Back? Why It Matters,"* June 29, 2012, accessed March 10, 2017 from https://www.psychologytoday.com/blog/cutting-edge-leadership/201206/are-you-type-or-b-personality

56. Ibid.

57. *Finding Normal,* directed by Brian Herzlinger, Pure Fix Entertainment, 2013, DVD, Vivendi Entertainment, USA, 2014.

58. Paige Dees, and Jason Dees. *"Great Marriage,"* Annual Promise Ministries Church Marriage Retreat, Gatlinburg, Tennessee, January 2017.

59. Hudson, *"25 Things,"* 2014.

60. Ibid.

61. *Inside Out*, directed by Pete Docter, Ronnie del Carmen & Andrew Coats, Pixar Animation Studios, DVD, Walt Disney Pictures, USA, 2015.

62. Riggio, *"Are you a Type A or B Personality?"* 2012.

63. McLeod, *"Type A Personality,"* 2014.

64. Hudson, *"25 Things,"* 2014.

65. *Woman's Study Bible*, ed. Dorothy Kelley Patterson and Rhonda Harrington Kelley, (Nashville: Thomas Nelson Publishers, 1995), 1188.

66. Women in the Bible, *Martha*, https://www.womeninscripture.com/martha/ (April 2, 2018).

67. Kathryn L. McCance, Sue E. Huether, Valentina L. Brashers, and Neal S. Rote, *Pathophysiology: The Biologic Basis for Disease in Adults and Children*, 6th ed. (Maryland Heights, MO: Mosby Elsevier, 2010), 337.

68. McCance, et al., *Pathophysiology*, 337.

69. Elizabeth Scott, *"Type A Personality Traits; What Does It Mean to Have A Type A Personality?"* Last modified 2016, accessed March 10, 2017 from http://www.verywell.com/type-a-personality-traits-3145240

70. Ibid.

71. McCance, et al., Pathophysiology, 339.

72. Ibid. 339-340.

73. Scott, *"Type A Personality Traits."*

74. *Turning Point*, David Jeremiah, May 13, 2015, aired on WHCB: The Blessing.

75. Holly Lucille, *"General Adaptation Syndrome (GAS) Stages,"* August 31, 2016, https://www.integrativepro.com/Resources/Integrative-Blog/2016/General-Adaptation-Syndrome-Stages (July 1, 2017).

76. McCance, et al., *Pathophysiology*, 338.

77. Deane Alban, *"Norephinephrine: A Key Player In Stress, Depression, And ADHD,"* March 9, 2016, accessed June 11, 2017 from http://www.reset.me/story/norepinephrine-a-key-player-in-stress-depression-and-adhd/

78. Lucille, *"GAS Stages."*

79. Alban, *"Norephinephrine."*

80. McCance, et al., *Pathophysiology*, 355.

81. Alban, *"Norephinephrine."*

82. Lucille, *"GAS Stages."*

83. Alban, *"Norephinephrine."*
84. Ibid.
85. University Health News (UHN), *"Surprising Research Challenges Our Understanding of Norepinephrine Deficiency and Natural Remedies for Depression,"* September 12, 2016 http://universityhealthnews.com/daily/depression/surprising-research-challenges-our-understanding-of-norepinephrine-deficiency/ (accessed June 11, 2017)
86. Ibid.
87. McCance, et al., *Pathophysiology*, 338-339.
88. Ibid. 339.
89. Kendra Cherry, *"The Role of the Conditioned Response in Classical Conditioning,"* reviewed by Steven Gans, MD, last modified June 8, 2018, https://www.verywellmind.com/what-is-a-conditioned-response-2794974 (June 23, 2018).
90. Ibid.
91. Ibid. 343.
92. McCance, et al., *Pathophysiology*, 339-349.
93. Centers for Disease Control and Prevention (CDC), *"Heart Disease,"* last modified August 15, 2015, http://www.cdc.gov (June 24, 2017).
94. McCance, et al., *Pathophysiology*, 347.
95. GB HealthWatch, *"Genes and Me; Type A Personality,"* http://www.gbhealthwatch.com/Trait-TypeA-Personality.php (July 1, 2017)
96. Ibid.
97. L. Sirri, et al., *"Type A Behaviour,"* September 2012.
98. Ibid.
99. Steve Tovian, et al., *"Stress effects on the body,"* http://www.apa.org/helpcenter/stress-body.aspx June 11, 2017).
100. McCance, et al., 339-349.
101. Centers for Disease Control and Prevention (CDC), *"Depression,"* last modified March 30, 2016, http://www.cdc.gov/mentalhealth/basics/mental-illness/depression.htm (July 2, 2017).
102. Ibid.
103. Laura Pratt, and Debra J. Brody, *"Depression in the U.S. Household Population, 2009-2012," NCHS Data Brief*, no. 172, (December 2014), Hyattsville, MD: National Center for Health Statistics, http://www.cdc.gov/nchs/data/databriefs/db172.pdf (July 2, 2017).
104. McCance, et al., *Pathophysiology*, 657.

105. P.H.I.L. Foundation, 2013.
106. McCance, et al., *Pathophysiology*, 353.
107. Tovian, et al., *"Stress Effects."*
108. Ibid.
109. American Psychological Association (APA), *"Gender and Stress,"* 2010, http://www.apa.org/news/press/releases/stress/2010/gender-stress.aspx (July 2, 2017).
110. Ibid.
111. Ibid.
112. Ibid.
113. United States of Department of Labor (USDOL), *"Mothers and Families,"* last modified August 2014, http://www.dol.gov/wb/stats/mother_families.htm (July 1, 2017)
114. McCance, et al., *Pathophysiology*, 349-351.
115. Tovian, et al., *"Stress Effects."*
116. McCance, et al., *Pathophysiology*, 354.
117. Ibid.
118. Saul McLeod, *"Stress Management,"* last modified 2015, https://www.simplypsychology.org/stress-management.html (September 4, 2017).
119. Ibid.
120. Ibid.
121. Ibid.
122. McCance, et al., *Pathophysiology*, 355.
123. Lucille, *"GAS Stages."*
124. McLeod, *"Type A Personality,"* 2014.
125. Ibid.
126. McCance, et al., *Pathophysiology*, 354.
127. Mayo Clinic, *"Biofeedback,"* last modified January 24, 2016, http://www.mayoclinic.org/tests-procedures/biofeedback/home/ovc-20169724 (June 24, 2017).
128. Ibid.
129. Scott, *"Type A Personality."*
130. Ibid.
131. Ibid.

132. Meri Wallace, *"The Effect of Birth Order on Children,"* May 31, 2016, http://www.google.com/amp/s/how-raise-happy-cooperative-child/201605/the-effect-birth-order-children%3famp, (February 10, 2018).

133. Rachel Macy Stafford, *"The Day I Stopped Saying 'Hurry Up'," Hands Free Mama*, July 16, 2013, www.handsfreemama.com/2013/07/16/the-day-i-stopped-saying-hurry-up/ (July 17, 2017).

134. Ibid.

135. Stafford, *"The Day."*

136. Shalini Paruthi, MD, *"Common Causes, Effects, and Solutions to Sleep Deprivation in Children,"* November 13, 2015, http://www.sleepreviewmag.com/2015/11/common-causes-effects-solutions-sleep-deprivation-children/ (accessed February 10, 2018).

137. American Academy of Pediatrics, *"American Academy of Pediatrics Supports Childhood Sleep Guidelines,"* June 13, 2016, https://www.aap.org/en-us/about-the-aap/aap-press-room/Pages/American-Academy-of-Pediatrics-Supports-Childhood-Sleep-Guidelines.aspx (February 10, 2018).

138. Kim West, *"11 Negative Effects of Childhood Sleep Deprivation,"* 2018, https://sleeplady.com/toddler-sleep-problems/11-negative-effects-of-childhood-sleep-deprivation/ (February 10, 2018).

139. Shalini, *"Common Causes."*

140. Frank Powell, *"9 Things Your Children Need (But Won't Tell You)," Restoring Culture Through Christ*, February 19, 2016, http://www.frankpowell.me/things-children-need (April 26, 2017)

141. Ibid.

142. Ibid.

143. Ibid.

144. *The Woman's Study Bible*, p. 2028.

145. Ibid, p.1940.

146. Ibid.

147. Ibid.

148. Henry Brandt, *"5 Steps to Overcome Pride,"* http://www.biblicalcounselinginsights.com (June 5, 2017).

149. Ibid.

150. Ibid.

151. *The Woman's Study Bible*, p. 817.

152. Brandt, *"5 Steps."*

153. *The Woman's Study Bible*, p. 2077.

154. Ibid., p. 1165.
155. Ibid., p. 1790.
156. Dan Hayden, *"A Peculiar People-1 Peter 2:9,"* http://www.awordfromtheword.org/a-peculiar-people (May 29, 2017).

ACKNOWLEDGMENTS

To all of my co-workers from the emergency room, eye surgery center, and now women's health—I have created lifelong friendships with many of you, and continue to be awed by your knowledge and skills in caring for our communities. I have evolved into the nurse I am today because of each and every one of you. To my current supervising physician—Christy Stevens—I can never repay you for the knowledge I have gained working as your nurse practitioner. You are a woman after God's heart and have truly fulfilled your calling and talent by serving families within our community.

To my previous pastors and Sunday school teachers at McPheeters Bend Baptist Church, and First Baptist Church in Church Hill—I am privileged to have Hawkins County roots and pray for continued blessings as you bring souls to Christ.

Without a doubt, I know this book was meant to be written because God continued to provide during each stage of this process. Thank you to Cassie Kitzmiller for your early recommendations and for introducing me to SPS (Self-Publishing School). I have learned invaluable information for writing, marketing, launching, and publishing. To all the SPS team and members—thank you for all the guidance and encouragement! For more information on how to write your own book, please click on the link: https://xe172.isrefer.com/go/sps4fta-vts/bookbrosinc6344

A very special thank you to my initial readers—Becky, Jessica, and Christy—thank you for your creative criticism and for making this book even better than I could have imagined! Also, many thanks to my Uncle Michael for his artistic input and Ms. Christina Thomas at King University for mastering the design of my first book cover.

To my editor—Rachel McCracken—thanks for coping with my Type A traits during the editing phase. I could not have asked for a better partner to lead me on this new adventure, and I am eternally grateful for your Christian guidance throughout this process. And many thanks to my Launch Team for making this book a success from the beginning.

Finally, to my current Promise Ministries Church—the smallest church I have ever attended and yet, despite its size, this church is responsible for the exponential growth of my spiritual maturity. While attending this church, I read the Bible in its entirety and sang the first of many solos. My husband delivered the first of many sermons and our daughter gave her heart to Jesus during a very special vacation Bible school—a day we will never forget! Many thanks to Preacher Steve's guidance and for establishing our church's Type A Committee of which

I am a member. I am forever grateful to our church family for your many prayers and to our *"village"* who has helped us raise our daughter. And most importantly, it is in this church where I have gained wisdom leading me on this new, unfamiliar path as a Christian author. May the Lord continue to bless our little church as we continue to keep our eyes on Him!

ABOUT THE AUTHOR

Autumn lives in Tennessee with her husband, Rob, their daughter, Reese, and their three-year-old Cocker Spaniel, Charlotte. Autumn accepted Jesus Christ as her personal Savior at the age of ten years old and has been a professed Type A individual ever since she can remember. She has been a nurse for the last 17 years, and is a graduate of Walters State Community College and East Tennessee State University. She previously worked as a Certified Emergency Nurse at the third busiest Level I Emergency Room and Trauma Center in the state of Tennessee, and later as a pre-operative and circulating nurse at a local eye surgery center.

Upon receiving her master's degree as a nurse practitioner, she began her profession as a women's health care provider and continues to specialize in high risk obstetrics as well as gynecology. While enjoying a blessed career serving in her community, Autumn continues to serve as a teacher for the children's Sunday school class, sings on the church praise team, and operates the church's social media account—and participates on the church's notorious Type A committee.

Autumn enjoys cooking with her daughter and vacationing in between her husband's coaching seasons. She has never missed an episode of Fixer Upper, and she is always searching for new recipes on Pinterest. She and her family also enjoy cheering from the stands at various high school and college sporting events.

Be sure to look for her second book—*Type A Christian: Restoring Our Fruit*, where Autumn will discuss various obstacles in having a Type A personality within our Christian lives. She will teach you how to overcome these obstacles by transforming and restoring each of the nine attributes of the fruit with the help of the Holy Spirit.

Dear Readers,

I truly hoped you enjoyed reading Type A Christian. Again, it took nearly eight years to complete this first book as I knew God gave me a wonderful idea, and I didn't want to let Him down! Surprisingly, this first book was only half of my original manuscript!

That's right! I have already completed much of the second half of my next book, Type A Christian: Restoring Our Fruits. The second book will focus individually on the nine attributes of the fruit of the Spirit as we learn how to overcome various obstacles to become better fruit bearers.

I would love to hear your personal stories and how your Type A personalities have impacted the Church and your walk with Christ! Also, any recommendations for future topics regarding Type A Christian are most definitely welcomed! You can write me at TypeAChristian@gmail.com

Now, I have a quick favor to ask. Your feedback is very important! Additional reviews can actually improve access in allowing others to find this book easier online—how awesome would it be to help reach other Christians who are also Type A—or anyone wanting to improve their personality traits in their Christian walk! Please take a moment (or at least put it on your short-term to-do list!) and leave a review on ***Amazon*** *or* ***Goodreads****.*

Again, many thanks for reading! I have prayed over each of you to receive blessings as we serve others by using our fruit! ~ Galatians 5:22-23, Matthew 22:36-39, & Matthew 28:18-20 ~

Much Love, Autumn

NOW IT'S YOUR TURN

Discover the EXACT 3-step blueprint you need to become a bestselling author in 3 months.

Self-Publishing School helped me, and now I want them to help you with this FREE WEBINAR!

Even if you're busy, bad at writing, or don't know where to start, you CAN write a bestseller and build your best life.

With tools and experience across a variety niches and professions, Self-Publishing School is the only resource you need to take your book to the finish line!

DON'T WAIT

Watch this FREE WEBINAR now, and Say *"YES"* to becoming a bestseller:

https://xe172.isrefer.com/go/sps4fta-vts/bookbrosinc6344

Made in the USA
Columbia, SC
07 May 2020